Crete Walks in the Apokoronas

by

Geoff Needle

A collection of 25 selected walks around different parts of the Apokoronas region of North West Crete.

Crete Walks in the Apokoronas

First edition: 2011

Copyright © Geoffrey Needle 2011

ISBN: 978-1-4475-1260-8

All rights reserved.

The moral rights of the author have been asserted in accordance with the Copyright, Designs and Patents Act 1988 of the United Kingdom.

No part of this publication may be reproduced, stored in a retrieval system, or transmitted or recorded in any form or by any means, without the prior permission in writing of the Author.

****

Every care has been taken to give complete and accurate directions for all the walks in this book. They are described as they were when walked in 2009 or 2010. The author takes no responsibility for any changes that have occurred in those areas since that time.

The author takes no responsibility for any accident or injury that may occur to any walkers on any of these walks, however it may be caused.

Walkers must accept full responsibility for their own safety and that of other members of their party at all times.

****

Graphic of the Apokoronas Region:
Courtesy of Wikipedia, Author "Mtiedemann" under Licence GFDL.

****

Correspondences to email address: apokoronaswalks@yahoo.com

Crete Walks in the Apokoronas

CONTENTS

	Page
Starting Points of Walks	4
Introduction	5
Notes on the Use of Walk Directions	28
Safety Notes	32

The Walks	Length (kms)	Average Time (hrs)	
1. Agioi Pantes - Fres	6.5	2.5	34
2. Alikambos - South East	12	3	38
3. Aptera - Greek, Roman, Turkish Ruins	6	2	41
4. Armeni - Orange Groves - River	6/10	2/3	45
5. Drapanos - Eastern Coastline	7	2.5	50
6. Embrosneros – North East	6	2	53
7. Fres - North East	9	3	58
8. Fres - Top Churches	2/4	1/2	63
9. Gavalohori - Douliana	8	3	66
10. Georgioupolis - Beach	6	2	71
11. Kaina - South East	5	1.5	75
12. K. Alexandrou - K. Amygdalou	3.5/7	1.5/2.5	79
13. Kokkino Horio – North East	8	2.5	83
14. Melidoni - Foothills	17	5	87
15. Mouri (near Kournas Lake) - East	5	1.5	91
16. Neo Chorio - Macheri - Nerochori	7.5/9	2.5/4	94
17. Nippos - South East	5/7	1.5/2	101
18. Permonia - Fres	7	2.5	106
19. Plaka - Coastline	4/6	1.5/2	110
20. Ramni - Foothills - Two Churches	3.5/8	1.5/2.5	113
21. Stylos - Diktamos Gorge	6/9.5	1.5/3	117
22. Vafes - Vothonas Plateau - Foothills	12	3.5	124
22A. Vothonas Plateau (Short Walk)	7	2	128
23. Vamos - South West	8	2.5	129
24. Vamos Old Village - North West	4/5.5	1.5/2	133
25. Xirosterni - Kefalas	6	2	138

Crete Walks in the Apokoronas

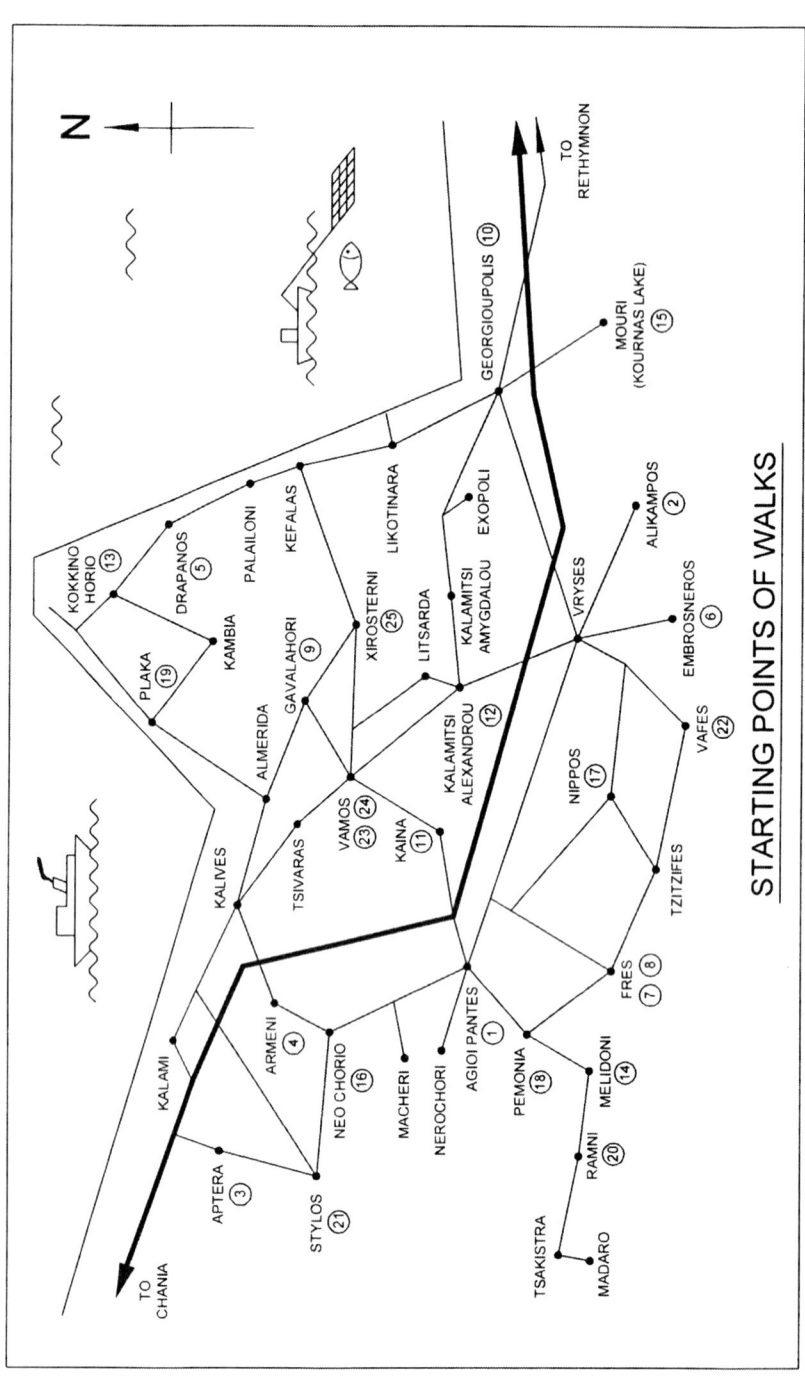

Crete Walks in the Apokoronas

INTRODUCTION

The Apokoronas region of North West Crete, although relatively small in size compared to the whole of the island, has areas of great diversity that make it a great place to walk around. The 25 selected walks in this book will take you to different parts of the region so that you can see and enjoy this wide diversity.

The region has a varied coastline ranging from fine sandy beaches which are havens for summer tourists, to deserted rocky headlands with caves and cliffs. The White Mountains tower over the whole area, hiding small mountain villages that have so far escaped the ravages of modern development.

Between the White Mountains and the coast there varying terrains with lots of tracks that are ideal for walking. There is a large and completely flat area of olive and citrus groves (orange, lemon, grapefruit and mandarin) irrigated with water from underground springs, streams or rivers that find their way down from the mountains to the sea. There are other areas of gently undulating terrain with olive and avocado groves, as well as areas with gorges and cuttings that carve their way down from the White Mountains to the sea.

On the fringes of the Apokoronas region there are areas that remain stark and barren, with boulders and rocks spread around patches of grass and scrub. Some of these areas, although we might consider them to be wild and inhospitable today, still support a number of working sheep and goat farms that are just about managing to provide a subsistence livelihood for their 'hardy' farmers whose families might have been working and tending those areas for many generations. These farmers will be making good use of any old, disused, stone shepherds' huts or animal shelters that have remarkably survived on their land over the centuries. Most of these old stone structures have been dismantled over the years to recycle their valuable stone into the construction of more modern properties. These old stone structures, where they still exist, bear silent witness to the very hard lives that must have been lived by their earlier inhabitants.

Crete Walks in the Apokoronas

There are many small churches and chapels to be found all over the Apokoronas region that remain unlocked for you to visit. Some of these are located in such isolated and difficult to reach places that you could not imagine yourself finding one there. A few of these small churches are relatively new or still under construction but the vast majority of them are very old. It is remarkable that a number of these old churches still have areas of their inside walls displaying large portions of the original colourful frescos that once adorned them, despite the ravages of the centuries that have elapsed since they were first painted.

It is perhaps even more surprising to enter one of these small and isolated churches, maybe down a deep gorge, in a cave or on top of a hill, to find a candle or olive oil lamp still burning inside, showing that it is still being cared for and used for worship by its local communities. This, in a small way, seems to connect you with those devoted people.

Typical Small Church Interiors

Each church is dedicated to its own particular patron saint and each saint has their own special Saints Day on which a service will be held in the church to celebrate the life of that saint. It is always worth trying to enter these small churches if the opportunity arises as you never know what you are going to find inside them. Even the plainest looking church on the outside can be beautifully decorated inside.

With so many interesting villages, small hamlets and churches, tavernas and kafenions, each having their own individual character, and a landscape with views that change so quickly within a short distance, a drive along roads or lanes in the Apokoronas region that you haven't been on before can become an exciting adventure. If you are a tourist in the area, a casual and aimless drive through the region can give you memories and photographs to cherish.

Crete Walks in the Apokoronas

However this book is not about driving, other than getting to the starting points for each walk, it is about walking. The 25 walks in this book have been specially put together to take the walker through what the author has found to be some of the quietest parts of the Apokoronas region, having some of the best countryside, and/or some of the best views. The walk descriptions are fully detailed so walkers can enjoy the tranquillity, the scenery, and the views without becoming lost in an area of countryside they do not know.

****

The Apokoronas region of North West Crete covers approximately 200 square kilometres and lies halfway between the large towns of Chania and Rethymnon. It consists mostly of the triangular promontory that lies between Georgioupolis in the east, Aptera in the west, the mouth of Souda bay in the north, and the northern foothills of the White Mountains in the south, plus a little further beyond. Vamos is considered to be its capital and lies almost at its geographic centre. The three main towns of the region are Vamos, Armeni and Vryses.

The White Mountains

The White Mountain range of western Crete, or the Lefka Ori as it is more correctly known, is one of three significant mountain ranges that are spread along the island of Crete. The other two mountain ranges are those of Mount Ida (Psiloritis) in central Crete and Mount Dhikti in eastern Crete.

The White Mountains are appropriately named as they wear a picturesque cap of snow that stretches all across their tops from December to May, and sometimes into June. There are reputed to be over 40 gorges and over 25 peaks spread over the mountain range. The highest peak is called Pachnes which is currently at 2454m above sea level. It is just beaten into second place by the highest summit on Crete which is that of Mount Ida (Psiloritis) at 2456m. The highest peak of Mount Dhikti is 2147m.

Crete Walks in the Apokoronas

The three mountain ranges of Crete are being formed by the very slow collision of two tectonic plates, the European plate and the African plate. This slowly continuing geological process is increasing their heights at a rate of approximately 2mm a year. It is also the reason why Crete is prone to the occasional earthquake or tremor.

As impressive as they may look from anywhere within the Apokoronas region, at best you are only seeing the lower foothills of the White Mountain range. The vast bulk of the White Mountain range lies between the centre of the island and the south coast where huge areas lie well above an altitude of 2000m. Being so high and so close to the sea, they have a significant effect on the weather patterns of the region.

The upper slopes of the White Mountains, above the snow line, are mostly barren with pine and cypress trees clinging to the slopes. The walking terrain is hostile and not one for any but the most experienced walkers and climbers, although mountain goats don't seem to have too much of a problem!

The lower slopes and foothills of the White Mountains are more fertile and support a number of small rural communities with goat and sheep farming. Sustaining life in these small villages and hamlets can be very difficult, especially in the depths of winter with the heavy snows and rains. These mountain villages are the places where you still find the 'real' Cretan spirit of dogged determination and grit, of not to be beaten by the elements, where the people have great resilience and stoicism to withstand such adverse conditions year after year without giving in. They are where you see life as it really was before the 4x4 pick-up truck took over from the donkey. Maybe that is why you do not see many new villas with swimming pools being built in those areas.

One of the nicest views in the Apokoronas region is to be seen on a clear day in spring when looking towards the White Mountains. The white snow covering the undulating tops of the mountains will be set against a clear blue sky above and the foothills below, their slopes and small peaks covered with verdant fresh foliage of various shades of green, with the dark green dots of cypress trees and the white dots of small villages. At all other times of the year the White Mountains will still command your attention and demand your respect. They are very deceiving, always being much larger and much further away than they appear. The foothills of the White Mountains have some superb scenery, but the walks in them are generally not easy.

Crete Walks in the Apokoronas

Although these walks do reward the effort made. The small villages that cling to its hillsides or hide in its small valleys are also well worth exploring. The White Mountains form a very picturesque backdrop to most of the walks in this book, three of which (14, 20, 22) venture up into their lower foothills and provide splendid views of the scenery below and much further beyond.

The White Mountains in Spring

Drapanos Hill

Another significant geographic feature dominating the Apokoronas region is Drapanos Hill (527m), the large, almost flat-topped hill perched on the end of the eastern side of the Apokoronas triangle. It also forms a picturesque backdrop to most of the walks in this book. The eastern 'hidden' side of the hill is relatively barren and drops down to a rocky coastline, while the other three sides drop down to a number of villages. One of these villages, Kokkino Horio, featured in the 1964 film "Zorba the Greek" with Anthony Quinn, along with Stavros on the far side of the Akrotiri peninsula, but you would probably not recognise it in the film now since that village, and the two neighbouring villages of Plaka and Kambia, have seen much development over recent years.

Crete Walks in the Apokoronas

Drapanos Hill

The rocky coastline at the northern end of Drapanos Hill falls down to a couple of coves and sea caves, with a small lighthouse perched on the far corner at the mouth of Souda bay. The top of the hill has a number of masts for various electronic communication systems. Drapanos Hill is not normally accessible to casual walkers, despite the tempting track that can be seen climbing up its western side with a round water tank half way up, since very near the bottom is a fence and locked gate.

Three walks in this book (5, 13, 19) take you around different parts of the Drapanos Hill area.

Aptera Hill and Zourva Hill

The western end of the Apokoronas region is visually dominated by the small Turkish fortress perched on top of a low hill near the modern village of Aptera. At an altitude of 187m above sea level the fortress looks over Souda bay in a northerly direction and the citrus groves of the flat Armeni plain in a south easterly direction. That low hill is dwarfed by the second much higher hill which is seen immediately behind it to the west. This is called Zourva Hill and rises to 610m.

Although Zourva Hill is just outside the Apokoronas region, it remains a very prominent geographic feature that can be seen from most locations within it. It has a broad flat-topped profile, very much like a mirror-image of Drapanos Hill, and together they almost look like a pair of bookends with the Apokoronas region packaged in the middle.

Crete Walks in the Apokoronas

The next low hill, just inland from and adjacent to the Turkish fort, was once encircled by a stone wall 3.5km long. This wall surrounded the ancient Greek city of Aptera that was founded in the 7th century BC. It grew to become an important commercial and political centre through the pre-Hellenic and Hellenic (500-300 BC) periods, and it even minted its own coins. Only small ruined sections of that wall remain now.

The Romans were the next inhabitants of the walled hill. They built extensively over the old Greek city and have left their mark today in the form of some splendid ruins that still amaze us today through the scale of their civil engineering, the most impressive being the immense three-section vaulted underground water cistern. The hill was inhabited until the 7th century AD when an earthquake destroyed it.

The more recent Turkish occupation of Crete (1669-1898) has also left its mark in Aptera with two fortresses that are still almost intact today. The first fort is the one on top of the hill and already mentioned. The second fort, a much larger one, is located directly below the first fort on a small plateau near the waters of Souda bay. It found use more recently as a prison for political dissidents between 1967-1974. Today both forts are peaceful, the only noise coming from the traffic on the National Highway that squeezes its way between them.

Zourva Hill towering over Aptera Hill

Walk (3) in this book takes in all the features of ancient Aptera.

11

Crete Walks in the Apokoronas

Kournas Lake

The eastern end of the Apokoronas region has the only natural freshwater lake on Crete, the near circular Kournas Lake. The lake is picturesquely surrounded by hills, averages about 1000m in diameter and goes down to a depth of 22m. It is a lively place for visitors during the summer months, having a number of tavernas and gift shops and a safe shallow eastern shoreline that is suitable for bathing.

The far side of the lake is reserved for a wide range of wildlife and is inaccessible. The lake area supports a large diverse range of flora and fauna throughout the year, especially in the spring and summer months.

One walk (15) in this book goes into the countryside near the lake, making a visit to the lake an easy option to take afterwards.

Other Areas

The almost flat area between Kournas Lake and the village of Alikambos (Walk 2) looks more like the barren landscape of the eastern end of Crete, beyond Sitia, but it still supports a small number of thriving sheep and goat farms.

The Armeni plain (Walks 4, 21), between the villages of Armeni, Neo Chorio, and Stylos, is flat and fertile. It is covered with many olive and citrus groves (orange, lemon, grapefruit and mandarin). Located in amongst these groves is the complete shell of an old Byzantine church that somehow seems completely out of place there. Numerous natural water wells are to be found around the groves of the Armeni plain.

The areas in and around Stylos village (Walk 21), as well as having the olive and citrus groves already mentioned, have underwater springs that bubble up from the ground below. These produce flowing streams that are a pleasure to see, especially in the hot summer months. Some of those springs have been exploited by the large water bottling plant in Stylos village. The chances are that you have already drunk some of their "Samaria" bottled water which is distributed far and wide.

All along the northern coastline of the region (Walks 13, 19) there are great views looking across to Souda bay and the Akrotiri peninsula beyond. You can watch the tourist planes landing and taking off at Chania airport which is on the plateau the other side of Souda bay.

Crete Walks in the Apokoronas

A separate area of Chania airport belongs to the Greek Air Force. You can often see and hear its modern Lockheed Martin F16 jet fighter planes flashing passed or practicing manoeuvres in the skies above.

Souda bay is a port of call for warships of the NATO alliance. It is not unusual to see the grey frigates, submarines, supply ships, or the occasional aircraft carrier, slowly sailing into or out of port. They moor up at the navy dockyard on the south coast of the Akrotiri peninsula.

Large white ANEK ferry ships regularly come into Souda bay to moor up at the Souda ferry terminal. They make their daily round trips to and from Piraeus, arriving in the mouth of Souda bay around 5.00 in the morning and sailing out of the bay around 9.30 in the evening. The first indication you have of them is the slow thumping of their large engines.

Vamos is the administrative capital of the Municipality of Vamos, which consists of many of the surrounding villages. It has funding from the European Union that helps support a group of local businessmen in a successful project to preserve the traditional crafts and products of the region and to restore many of the old stone buildings using traditional materials and crafts and to turn them into guest houses.

Vamos is a thriving small town that retains much of its traditional character. You can still walk along some old cobbled roads in the old part of Vamos and through its narrow lanes of old properties that give testament to the wealth the village had in days gone by (Walk 24).

One of the best and longest sandy beaches in Crete runs for at least 6km from the village of Georgioupolis (Walk 10) towards Rethymnon, with its numerous small streams running into the sea. The busy village of Georgioupolis has a fishing harbour and many other attractions.

The twin villages of Kalamitsi Amygdalou and Kalamitsi Alexandrou are each located at the top of their own small gorge (Walk 12), while one of the largest and longest gorges in the Apokoronas region lies not far from Stylos (Walk 21).

Many other smaller villages around the Apokoronas region are also well worth visiting. A number of them are included in these walks, a few being: Macheri that nestles under a high cliff (Walk 16), Douliana with its traditional kafenion (Walk 9), and Embrosneros with the ruins of its old castle and superb cave church (Walk 6), to name but a few.

Crete Walks in the Apokoronas

The walks in this book, including those already mentioned, will pass through quiet areas of countryside, many with small churches and/or great views along their way.

Flora

The countryside around the Apokoronas region has trees of cypress, wild almond, carob, laurel, bay, olive, fig, pear, and a number of different types of oak. There are thorny brooms, sage, thyme and many other wild herbs. There are also many different types of orchid and iris to be found in the woods and hedgerows. In late winter and spring, after the rains, the countryside bursts into colour with the flowering of many different types of wild flora, many of which are native to Crete alone. The island will then be at its greenest and carpeted with many species of colourful flowers, almond trees will be in full blossom, the winter citrus trees will be full of fruit, and there will be all shades of red, pink and violet anemonies in the fields and grassland along with blue lupins. As the hot summer weather approaches many of those wild flowers will disappear, to be gradually replaced by brown dried grasses and twigs which can become a potential fire risk.

If a bush fire does happen to develop, which fortunately is not very often, the giant white Russian helicopter (R06293, Type: Mi-26T) that is based at Chania airport will be sent out to help extinguish it. It will hover over the sea, filling the large bucket it has suspended below with water, before conveying it to the seat of the fire where it is then dropped in one gush, breaking up into a spray as it falls. It might take many trips before a large fire is finally extinguished.

The Mi-26T Helicopter on Fire Duty

Crete Walks in the Apokoronas

As the damp colder weather of autumn and winter arrives, the tall spikes of the common asphodel, which can reach a height of 1m, will start shooting up from large bulbs just below the surface ready to display their delicate pinkish white flowers through till summer.

Another Greek tradition is the collecting the edible leaves from wild plants in the countryside, usually during winter and spring, and especially after rainfall. Men and women may be seen bending down and rummaging around in olive groves and hedgerows with plastic bags looking for these leaves that are termed 'horta'. The leaves are taken home to be boiled, steamed, fried, or even eaten raw, to produce a nutritious supplement to other vegetables, or to be used in traditional recipes such as pies. There are many wild plants that have edible leaves and it is important to know which they are before picking them. The following are some of the common plants, many we consider as weeds, that have edible green leaves that are classed in Crete as 'horta': fennel, corn poppy, dandelion, stingy nettle, borage and common mallow.

Birds

Crete, being an island that is surrounded by large areas of sea on all sides, is not on the migration routes of some species of birds, but it still hosts a large number of seasonal visitors, as well as having its own large and diverse range of resident species.

In the Apokoronas region you will be see buzzards soaring on the thermals, often being chased in aerial dog-fights by black and grey hooded crows. Kestrels hover stationary above the ground or sit on telegraph poles looking out for the movement of any tasty morsel hiding in the scrub below. The larger and more spectacular golden eagles and Griffin vultures may be seen in the higher foothills of the White Mountains, and then only if you are very lucky.

At lower levels, stonechats dart in and out of the dry stone walls looking for insects. An assortment of different finches, tits, sparrows and blackbirds can be seen flying around, flapping in the dry dust or dipping in the pools and puddles of tracks and gardens, while swifts and martins may be soaring above scooping up airborne insects. Doves and pigeons are also common birds to be seen in the countryside areas. Skylarks are more likely to be heard singing in the skies above rather than you being able to see them. Crete is a bird-watchers paradise when conditions are right with many more species than can be listed here.

Crete Walks in the Apokoronas

Weather

If you are going to be walking in the Apokoronas region it is a good idea to have some appreciation of the unusual weather patterns that can sometimes exist in the area. At best it might help you to avoid getting caught in a heavy rain shower when out in the open countryside. These patterns are partly caused by the geography of the area, where the Apokoronas region is effectively boxed in by a high hill on each side and the very high White Mountains behind, with the open mouth of the box facing out to sea.

The Apokoronas region, like the rest of Crete, has a warm Mediterranean climate. Summers are hot and dry with clear blue skies. Seasonal breezes from the north provide a welcome respite in the summer to make the hot days pleasantly tolerable. The higher mountain areas are cooler. The weather through the summer remains settled.

Winters are mild at the lower levels, with frost and snow being rare. Snow is not unknown right down to sea level. There are periods of strong winds, heavy rain, and spectacular thunderstorms that can flash all around. Most times the lightning will be accompanied, as you would expect, with the loud sound of thunder. Sometimes the lightning will occur far out at sea, many kilometres beyond the Akrotiri peninsula, although it will still look quite close such is its intensity. During those lightning storms far out to sea, quite eerily there will be no sounds of thunder at all. This is when you might consider relaxing for a while to sit back and watch one of nature's most magnificent spectacles.

The autumn, winter and spring winds in the Apokoronas region can be very changeable, with the following situations being quite common:

- High clouds moving in one direction with the ground winds moving in the opposite direction,

- The ground winds changing direction completely within minutes,

- One minute the ground winds are calm, the next minute they are gusting very strongly, and the next minute all is calm again.

The autumn, winter and spring rains can pour down continuously for many days without a break, or come and go within minutes. Rainbows can also be spectacular.

Crete Walks in the Apokoronas

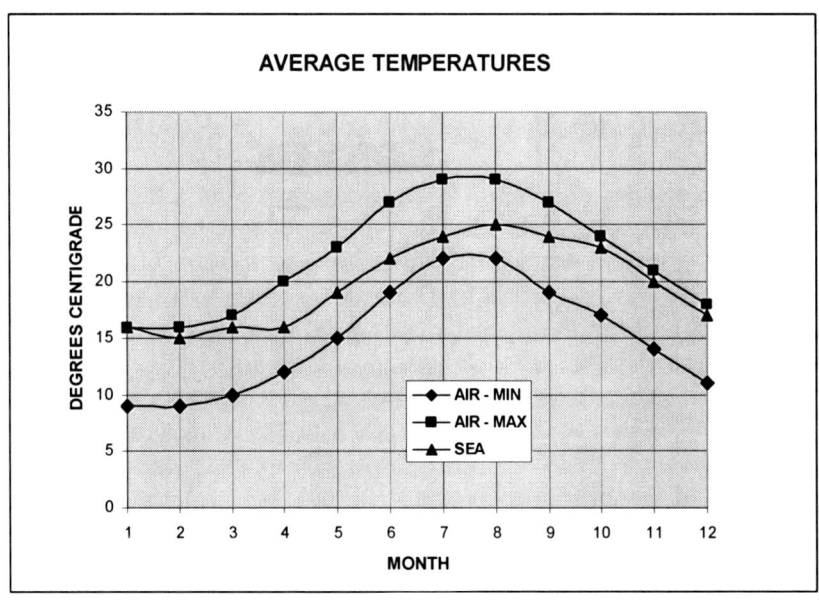

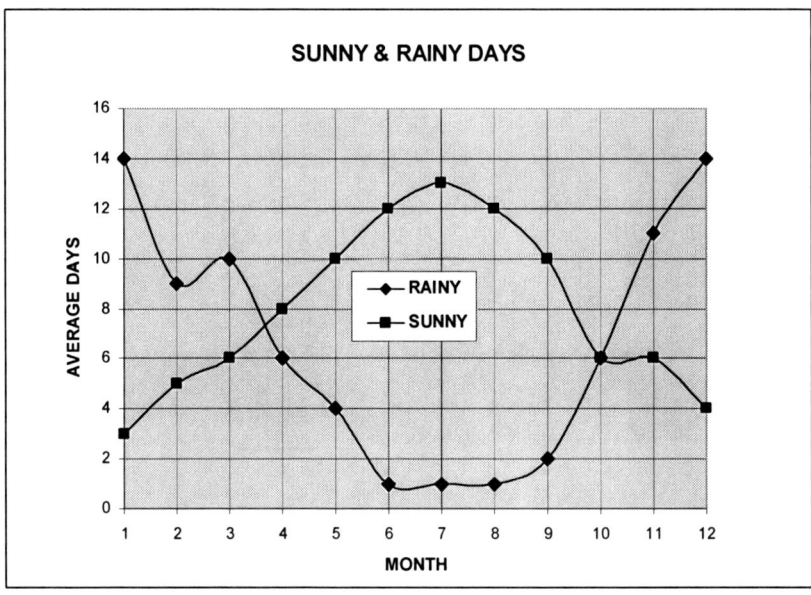

Rumbles of thunder can often be heard coming from somewhere across the top of the White Mountains from a lightning storm occurring far off in the distance. If the wind is blowing towards the sound of the thunder, then you can relax.

Crete Walks in the Apokoronas

If the wind is blowing from the same direction as the thunder and the clouds overhead start becoming dark or almost black, then gardens are certain to get a good watering in the very near future and if you are out walking in the countryside you are also going to get a good soaking.

The horror of local people in the Apokoronas region is the 'red rain'. These rains occur occasionally during the winter months when an exceptionally strong warm wind blows up from the south, known as a Sirocco wind. Before reaching Crete the Sirocco wind might have already passed over the Sahara desert picking up a load of red dust from the hot sands, and certainly passed over the Libyan Sea picking up a load of moisture. Before reaching the region it will also have passed over the cold high altitudes of the White Mountains, made even colder when they are covered with winter snow. This causes moisture in the Sirocco wind to start condensing out. This produces a characteristic and well-defined narrow cloud formation going from east to west over the region. This cloud formation is known locally as the 'Tongue'.

The 'Tongue' Cloud – Harbinger of a Heavy Storm

A cloud of a similar shape to the 'Tongue' can occur at any time of year when the wind blows from the south, even against a blue or lightly clouded sky, but they will not be as narrow or as sharply-defined, the winds will not be as strong, and they will not produce any rain. Only in winter, when the skies become heavily and darkly overcast with the south wind becoming very strong and gusting, that the narrow 'Tongue' cloud forms and the risk of heavy rains becomes a certainty.

Crete Walks in the Apokoronas

Within hours of the 'Tongue' appearing overhead the Sirocco wind gains even more strength accompanied by even stronger gusts. Soon afterwards the heavy rains start to fall. If the Sirocco wind did not pass over the Sahara desert to pick up red dust there will only be very heavy and prolonged rain. If it did happen to pick up red dust over the Sahara desert the rain produced will carry it down inside the raindrops. All external surfaces that get rained upon will be covered with a layer of that fine red dust. In swimming pools the clear water will go cloudy, the white grout between the tiles will go pink, and after the dust has settled there will be a layer of red slurry on the bottom of the pool. The rains and winds can last for several days. After the 'red rain' has stopped and everything has dried out, the cleanup operation to remove the red dust can commence. The red dust is as fine as talcum powder.

If you are out walking out in the countryside and the weather deteriorates, and you notice the 'Tongue' cloud forming along the edge of the White Mountains, the wind getting very strong and gusting, and dark clouds appearing overhead from over the mountains, you might be well advised to start thinking about heading for shelter or terminating the walk unless you are determined and have good rainwear with you.

As bad as the cool and damp seasonal winter weather can sometimes be, it is usually broken up by the very welcome 'halcyon days'. These are days when a strange calm descends over Crete, bringing with it 7-10 days of clear sunny days. The halcyon days can occur anytime between December and February. After they have passed, the days of heavy rain and strong winds will return. The halcyon days account for the small dip seen in the graph of the average number of rainy days that occur during the winter months.

A typical year would see the following weather patterns:

<u>January and February</u>
The weather can be a frustrating combination of days that are cold or warm, of winds that are light or strong, of rains that can be light or heavy, of thunder and lightning or sun. A few days might be continuous rain and the next few days might be sun. Frost in Crete is very rare but there have been occasions when up to 60cm of snow has fallen over lower villages but it has all melted within a week. There have also been winters when the heavy rains have caused severe flash floods in the region. The settled halcyon days usually give a short but welcome respite to the bad winter weather of winds and rains.

Crete Walks in the Apokoronas

<u>March and April</u>
The weather is still unsettled, being either very sunny and warm, or very cool and wet. The nights are still cool or cold. The weather is generally improving towards the hotter sunny days of summer.

<u>May and June</u>
Settled warmer weather has almost arrived, getting hotter day by day but not too hot, with still the odd short rainy spells to spoil the party.

<u>July and August</u>
These are the hottest and driest months. Sometimes the days are too hot for comfort, but on most days a light cooling breeze coming off the sea makes things much more bearable. Many of the green grasses and shrubs of the spring landscape have turned to yellow, gold or brown. There is a potential for water shortages in some isolated areas.

<u>September and October</u>
The risk of having very hot days have passed, giving way to sunny slightly cooler days and much cooler evenings. The countryside remains dry and a potential fire risk, with bonfires still officially banned until the damp winter months.

<u>November and December</u>
The weather again becomes unsettled. Warmer days of sun are interspersed with cooler days of cloud, wind and rain. The nights are getting colder. Thunder and lightning storms become more frequent and fierce. It might be a good time to order oil for the heating system.

Water

In the past the Apokoronas region suffered badly from a lack of reliable sources of natural water. This limited any long-lasting and worthwhile agricultural activity and resulted in a severe reduction in the population over time. Therefore the smaller old villages did not grow and were able to retain their individual 'period' character and identity. Their surrounding rural landscapes were likewise unaffected by similar developments that were taking place in other areas. This trend has recently been reversed due mainly to foreigners that have come over to buy those old properties, or spare plots of land near them to build upon, in order that they can settle down here or to use as holiday homes. Some of the new owners have chosen to retain the Cretan character of the old properties and some have chosen to modernise them.

Unfortunately, the recent changes have occurred at a quicker rate than the improvements made to the old water infrastructure to enable it to cope with them. Consequently it is not unusual in some of the older villages and outlying areas to find there are occasional water shortages, especially during the summer months.

There are two types of water on Crete, the 'town' water and the 'agricultural' water. Both types of water are metered.

Town water comes from the supply authority and is treated, as you would expect, for domestic consumption. Agricultural water is not.

Agricultural water is collected from the springs, streams and rivers that are formed from the melting snow in the mountains or after heavy rains. It is pumped up into large round concrete storage tanks of 40m diameter that are located at high spots around the countryside. The water is then gravity-fed or pumped out for distribution around the area through many water standpipes, most being uniquely numbered.

Final distribution is achieved through an array of black plastic water pipes. Most of these pipes run over the ground, since there are so many areas of hard rock, stones and boulders in the subsoil that it is impractical to lay the pipes underground. The joints in these pipes often leak, so it is not unusual to find a pool of water where you would not expect to find one, like a wet section of road in mid summer.

'Agricultural' water is used on a large scale to irrigate citrus, avocado and olive groves and feed livestock, and on a smaller scale to top-up swimming pools and water gardens.

Electricity

The closest power stations generating electricity for the Apokoronas region are in Souda and Rethymnon. The power is transmitted through overhead lines running over hills and across fields to the main distribution points in towns and villages, and then to consumers.

This network of overhead power lines causes problems to consumers during thunder and lightning storms. The discharges of lightning often hit the power lines to cause frequent dips in the voltage or widespread blackouts. These blackouts can last for minutes, or for the rest of the day or night until any damage caused has been rectified.

Crete Walks in the Apokoronas

Sudden short and repeated voltage dips are a good warning that there is a lightning storm raging somewhere in the area even if its thunder cannot be seen or heard.

There is a risk of a lightning strike on any power line. This will produce an instantaneous high-voltage 'spike' that reaches across much of the supply system and any connected consumers. When this occurs, some types of electrical equipment that are connected to the power supply can become damaged, especially equipment containing sensitive electronic circuitry.

The same problem can occur if a telephone line is hit by lightning, where the telephone itself or any connected Internet modem can be instantly destroyed.

The lightning doesn't even have to strike a power or telephone line directly to cause the damage described. A lightning strike in close proximity to a power or telephone line can produce an electromagnetic pulse of high enough intensity that it can induce a similar high-voltage spike into the line that could then produce the same damaging effects.

If you are indoors and an approaching lightning storm is indicated by sudden short and repeated voltage dips, it is a good idea to unplug any sensitive electrical equipment. If you happen to find yourself in the centre of a violent thunder and lightning storm, it might be a good idea to also unplug other less-sensitive electrical equipment, or maybe, open the main switch to the property until the worst of the storm has passed over. You might have insurance, but prevention is better that cure.

Roads

It is only in the last 20 or so years, since tourism started to make a big impact on the everyday life of Crete, that the road infrastructure of the island has been significantly improved. Many of the minor tarmac roads and lanes in the Apokoronas region were originally rough country tracks.

Unfortunately, some of the tarmac roads and lanes received their top layer of tarmac before a solid foundation had been prepared underneath. As a result it is not uncommon for chunks of tarmac to be lifted off in places after heavy rains, leaving behind a deep hole into which car or motorcycle wheel can inadvertently drop.

Drivers and riders should always remain aware that there may be a deep hole anywhere in the tarmac road or lane ahead and make allowance for meeting one of these unexpectedly. They can then take avoiding action to prevent damage or injury.

Industries

The main industries of the Apokoronas are currently:

Agriculture - Olives

Crete is famous its tiny olives and has around 30 million olive trees. Although it cannot be confirmed it is believed that olive trees have been cultivated in Crete since before 1500 BC, during the Minoan period.

It is not surprising therefore that the traditional Cretan diet today uses olive oil, a monounsaturated fat, rather than other saturated or polyunsaturated fats or oils. The Cretan diet is regarded as one of the healthiest diets in Europe, helping to lower weight, reduce the effects of ageing and reduce blood pressure. Despite their small size, Cretan olives are packed with high quality oil. As they ripen they change colour from green to purple to black.

In the winter months of December to February teams of workers go out into the olive groves to lay netting around the base of each tree. Then with simple beaters or electric whirling machines they set about the back-breaking task of harvesting the olives into sacks. These are then taken to the local olive press for the production of some of the world's finest olive oil. Olive picking is often a family affair where all the members are roped in to help, the children and grandparents as well.

Modern olive presses receive the sacks of olives and tips them out into hoppers. The olives are then blown with jets of air to remove any loose twigs and leaves before being washed and passed through a crusher. The resulting lime-green pulp is passed through a centrifuge or press which squeezes out the emulsion of oil and water ready for the next process which separates out the water from the oil. The oil is finally put into containers ready to be collected by the supplier of the olives. Each batch of olives received by the press is numbered to ensure the oil produced gets back to the correct supplier. Each batch of oil is also tested for quality and a document printed which is given to the supplier.

Crete Walks in the Apokoronas

Agriculture of the Apokoronas Region (Oranges and Olives)

Olive oil from these small local presses is of high quality. Olive oil that has been produced by some larger manufacturers for mass consumption can be blended or have its chemical composition modified to reduce its natural acidity level and to increase profit margins. This has an adverse effect on its vitamin content, taste, smell and nutrition profile of the oil.

The best quality olive oil is termed 'Extra Virgin'. To be officially certified with this revered accolade it must not be modified in any way, it must be produced by a single, simple, cold pressing, and after testing it must have perfect flavour and odour, and an acidity of less that 1%.

Olives picked straight off the tree are hard and bitter so they need to be cured to remove their bitterness if they are to be used for eating. Many methods of curing olives have been developed over the centuries since they have been farmed. Each method favours a particular type of olive, whether they are green or black, small or large. Most of these methods will involve salt and are laborious and time consuming.

Olive trees grow very slowly, taking 5-7 years to produce their first fruit. When fully mature a large tree can produce up to 15 litres of oil in a good year. But there can also be bad years when the combination of sun, rain and wind come at the wrong time for pollination, or there are heavy rains and high winds that pull the ripe olives from the trees just before harvest time.

The evergreen olive tree also provides valuable wood that can be manufactured into furniture, intricately carved into ornaments or burned for heating. Its silvery green leaves can be fed to goats or used in medicinal teas for humans. Most of the olive oil produced in Greece is consumed within Greece, with the remainder being exported.

Crete Walks in the Apokoronas

Olive trees are almost indestructible, their large twisted contorted trunks bearing witness to them having had a very long life. Individual trees have supplied oil and wood to families over many centuries. In Vouves village (NW Crete) there is an amazing olive tree that is reputed to be about 3000 years old. It must be one of the first olive trees ever to have been planted in Crete, during the late Minoan period.

Agriculture – Oranges, Lemons, etc.

A large area of the Armeni plain is covered with citrus groves (orange, lemon, lime, grapefruit and mandarin), where most of the trees produce their ripe fruits in winter, although some bear fruit at other times. A walk through the groves in spring when the trees are in bloom is a delight, and in winter when the fruits are ripe is delicious!

Agriculture - Livestock

As in much of Greece, before the recent advent of mass tourism and building, farming of various kinds was the main occupation that sustained the inhabitants. Sheep and goat farming is still the main livestock industry, producing the milk required for another local industry, cheese making.

Livestock of the Apokoronas Region (Goats and Sheep)

One good sheep can produce a litre of milk per day for 6-7 months of the year. That's nearly 200 litres of milk per year. Six litres of milk are required to produce one kilo of cheese.

There are small cheese-making factories all over Crete, many of which are located in small villages to serve their local communities. The sheep and goats also produce other valuable commodities for their farmers, such as wool and lambs, meat and kids.

Crete Walks in the Apokoronas

Tourism

When Greece joined the European Communities on 1st January 1981 agriculture was still the main source of income for most Greeks and mass tourism was still in its infancy. The tourists then were more interested in visiting the classical sites like Athens, Delphi, Epidaurus, Olympia, etc. on the mainland, and Knossos and Phaistos on Crete.

The war in Yugoslavia during the early 1990's hastened the spread of mass tourism in Greece. Many northern European holiday makers found they had to seek out alternative destinations in which to lie out and bake in the sun. This sparked the start of rapid changes within Greece to accommodate the influx of new tourists, with their demands for improved holiday accommodation, better roads and services. Today Greece remains high up on the list of summer-sun destinations for mass tourism which brings in much needed income to all the tourist areas, and the country in general.

Building

Building is a trend of recent years. It has seen a rapid increase in the number of villas being built for northern Europeans, and for many Cretans who have become more affluent as a result of the increase in tourism. The Apokoronas region in particular has seen an above average concentration of these new properties and developments compared with other parts of Crete. Most of these have been built along the coastline or in the countryside and villages having quick and easy access to it.

All this development over the last 10 years or so has undoubtedly modified the rural nature of the region. It has changed its previous traditional Cretan character to become one of a busy cosmopolitan area with all the commercial services necessary to support it.

Despite the recent trend of increasing development in the Apokoronas region, there are still many areas that remain idyllic, that still retain their quiet rural identity against those modernising trends elsewhere.

The walks in this book are located in those quiet rural areas that still remain a pleasure to walk in.

Insects

The island of Crete has a wide variety of insects, many of which are quite harmless, but there is one that you should avoid a close encounter with, the scorpion. Around 25mm long, brown or black in colour, and

with a sting that is highly venomous. If you get stung by a scorpion seek medical attention at the earliest opportunity. They live in wood piles, heaps of stones, or in the crevices of dry stone walls. They do venture out of these so you should always be on your guard

for them. They will attack you if you are close and they feel threatened.

Mosquito flies come out at certain times of the year and during the cooler times of day in the summer. The preying mantis is usually brown in Crete and eats mostly live insects; they have wings but are seldom seen flying preferring, when not perched motionless waiting for prey, to scurry across the ground, walk along twigs or hang on walls. Wasps in Crete are quite docile compared with the more aggressive types found in some countries. They will not sting you unless provoked, so it is best not panic if they hover around you, just stay calm and they will soon move away, unless you take a swipe at them and miss!

There are many different species of grasshopper on the island of Crete, small and large. Each species has a long pair of back legs that help their males to produce their well known sounds for attracting a mate or

identifying other members of the same species. They do this by rubbing their hind legs, the inner sides of which have a row of small pegs, against the edge of the fore wings to produce an audible vibration, the pitch, sound, and rhythm of which varies according to the species.

One of the hallmarks of summer in Crete are the piercing, almost deafening, waves of cicada choruses screeching out from the trees as each cicada competes to be the loudest in its area.

Crete Walks in the Apokoronas

NOTES ON THE USE OF WALK DIRECTIONS

The various infrastructures in Greece are currently undergoing substantial, welcome and much needed improvements. The Apokoronas region is not lagging behind with these improvements.

It will therefore not be surprising to find a gravel track you have walked over one week will have had a layer of tarmac spread over it the next. This has made a precise description of some of these walks rather problematic, since a track might have been gravel when it was walked by the author, but by the time you read this book it might have become a tarmac lane, or even a tarmac road.

Therefore when reading the walk descriptions in this book, the terms "track", "lane" and "road" should be considered interchangeable. They were mostly correct when they were walked by the author in 2009.

The reason why many of the tracks are being upgraded with tarmac in this way is that the area is still very much a working agricultural landscape, relying heavily for its survival on the produce from olive and citrus groves, and from sheep and goat farming. Tourism alone does not support the area.

So what were once suitable surfaces for donkeys and carts in decades past are clearly no longer suitable for the 4x4 pick-up trucks which are the modern form of 'donkey' in the area.

The routes described in these walks will not be too adversely affected by these improvements, where they might have occurred, since they have been selected to be in the quietest parts of the countryside within the Apokoronas region. If anything they will probably make the walks a little easier to do, although it is still a shame to see nice country tracks disappear in this way. As they say - "That's progress".

To overcome this particular problem the layout and topography of junctions and turnings referred to in this book are fully described, as they would appear when you **arrive at or approach them**, and as they were seen when walked by the author in 2009. So if a track has been later laid with a covering of tarmac, the general layout and topography of the junction or turning should remain unchanged and should therefore still be as described, albeit with a different surface.

Crete Walks in the Apokoronas

To avoid any confusion over a particular junction or turning, they are fully described using the additional terms that are defined as follows:

- Ahead   A turning off the main track that goes forwards to some degree from the 'ahead' direction.
- Back   A turning off the main track that goes backwards to some degree from the 'ahead' direction.
- Bearing   A gradual bend in the track - it may be to left or right.
- Brow   A section of track that ascends over the top then descends.
- Dip   A section of track that descends to the bottom then ascends.
- Downhill   A gradient falling to some degree, but not level.
- Fork   A turning that departs from the main track you are on, but is not approximately 90° to the left or right, but is going either back or ahead to some degree.
- Left   A turning off left that neither goes back nor ahead.
- Off   A turning that departs from the main track you are on.
- Right   A turning off right that neither goes back nor ahead.
- Uphill   A gradient rising to some degree, but not level.

Examples: A turning off back left downhill.
            A fork ahead bearing right over a brow.
            A fork back left bearing left to a dip.

Therefore when you get to any junctions or turnings you should recognise them unambiguously from the descriptions of their topography. All this might sound a little complicated but it will not be when you read the descriptions at the junctions or turnings concerned.

Typical Numbered Water Standpipe

29

Crete Walks in the Apokoronas

The walk descriptions refer to prominent physical features you will encounter along the routes. These are given to help you confirm that you are going in the right direction. They are mostly water standpipes which usually have a number plate attached to them, but some do not.

They may also be small shrines, each telling a sad story of someone that has previously died at that spot. They are erected by loving family members or friends in their memory.

Other useful features referred to in the descriptions are signs that indicate when you are entering or exiting a village (see photos). Both these signs are blue/white/black. The 'exiting village' signs are additionally crossed with a red diagonal stripe.

'Entering Village' Sign (Blue/White)   'Exiting Village' Sign (With Red Stripe)

Distances to the next important junction or feature are given so that you know when to expect them. All distances given throughout the book are best estimates.

The times given throughout the book are also best estimates based on an average pace, but these times will greatly depend on the pace of individual walkers.

Junction that are passed along any given walk and which are going to be met again later in the same walk, are identified with (1), (2), etc. so they can be readily identified in the descriptions.

Where there is a suitable option for taking a short-cut, *these are described in italics and end with a reference **A**, **B**, etc*. These identifications refer to a later paragraph that will be similarly identified as ****A****, ****B****, etc. from which the walk directions then continue.

Crete Walks in the Apokoronas

The amount of detail given in these walk descriptions might seem excessive to some people, but there is a reason for that. The author has become lost on a number of occasions over the years, in the middle of nowhere and in a landscape he did not know, simply because the walk descriptions he was following were ambiguous or imprecise.

That situation can be very frustrating, especially when you have to double back unnecessarily, waste lots of time trying to unravel where you are or where you should be going, or have other people muttering "he's lost". Hopefully, the extra detail given in these walk descriptions will avoid those situations happening to other people.

If you happen to encounter any Greek dogs along the routes, they are almost always safely attached to a strong chain; the best advice is to ignore them. They do a lot of barking but are usually more afraid of you than you of them. They will soon lose interest in you after you have gone passed them.

Wire stock fences are erected at various places in the countryside. They may be permanent or temporary and are fastened shut using odd pieces of cord or wire. You can go through them provided there is not a padlock on them. Please ensure you leave them as you found them.

> *Any other useful and relevant information will be given in an indented paragraph in italic font – just like this one!*

Finally, all the walk directions in this book are given in good faith in the hope that they will remain correct when other people walk them later.

****

If you want to make a comment about the book, please send an email to:

apokoronaswalks@yahoo.com

****

Crete Walks in the Apokoronas

SAFETY NOTES

As many of these walks are out in open countryside there will not be places to get any refreshments until you get back into a village, so please take with you whatever you might require during the walk. Sweets and sugar drinks are helpful to keep your energy levels up. A picnic stop with something more substantial will keep you going on the longer walks.

Summer weather in Crete can be extremely hot, with the sun beating down all day. Be prepared in all ways for this, especially with an adequate supply of fresh water (you are sure to drink more than you think you will), the use of a high factor sun block, sunglasses and a sunhat. Early mornings and early evenings are cooler and less tiring if you do not like the heat of the day.

Spring and autumn weather in Crete is much like in the United Kingdom. The winter weather in Crete can be very wet if you are caught in a shower, so again, be prepared in all ways for this.

Always wear suitable and comfortable footware for walking over rocks and gravel paths – read the Terrain section of each walk before doing.

Mosquitoes, wasps and bees can be problems at certain times of the year, so have a tube of anti-histamine cream ready in case you are unlucky enough to get bitten by one.

It is wise to take a charged mobile phone with you.

If you are going to walk alone, do tell someone where you are going and when you expect to return.

Keep dogs on a lead where it might be deemed necessary or sensible as the penalties in Crete of a dog killing any livestock are severe. Clean up and dispose of any dog mess responsibly.

Please leave any gates and property as you find them.

The author takes no responsibility for any accidents that might occur to any walkers who go on any of these walks, however they may be caused. You must accept full responsibility at all times for both your own safety and that of other members of your party.

Crete Walks in the Apokoronas

Please do not:

- Leave any litter behind you as it can be both unsightly and a danger to wildlife.
- Drop any matches or smouldering cigarettes as they could start a huge and devastating fire, especially in dry weather.
- Damage or remove rocks, plants or trees as they are homes and food for insects, birds and animals.

Scorpions hide under stones, rocks and in wood piles. Their bite will more than likely render you in need of medical treatment within hours. They will not bother you if you don't bother them. Be aware of them and leave them alone.

Wild animals and farm animals can behave unpredictably, especially if they are with their young, so give them plenty of space.

Be wary of slippery surfaces on any paths, stones or tracks that are damp or wet, especially if they have green mould on them.

Think of yourself as an honoured guest on this lovely island of Crete and have due respect for the traditions and customs of the local people who are generous and friendly.

The most common pleasantry exchanged between passing Cretans is "yas-sas" and it is said with a smile. This means "health to you" or "cheers". It can also be used by you when casually passing a Cretan. Usually the first person will say "yas-sas" and the reply will be a short "ya". This simple courtesy made to a local Greek person costs nothing and you will get a warm smile back in return.

Other useful Cretan words or expressions you might use on a walk are:

Yes	- Nay.
No	- Oshi.
Please	- Parakalo.
Thank you	- Efkaristo.

Finally, you are here in Crete and have this book to hopefully enjoy the walks and to see some of the beautiful countryside that the Apokoronas region has to offer. I hope it helps you to do that.

Crete Walks in the Apokoronas

WALK 1

AGIOI PANTES – FRES

6.5 km – 2.5 hours

The Walk
This circular walk starts along a few short tracks to pass an old Turkish water spring before walking a short section of the Old National Road. The walk then takes much longer country tracks, with good views towards the White Mountains, to reach the village of Fres (pronounced Frey), before returning back along different country tracks.

The Terrain
The majority of this walk has moderate gradients over quiet tracks, but there is one very steep climb for 300m at 1.4km distance. After that the gradients are moderate all round. There is noticeable road noise from the New National Highway in the early and latter stages of the walk, but this is a small price to pay for the longer quieter tracks.

The Start
If heading from Vamos:
Proceed along the road from Vamos to Agioi Pantes. Cross the bridge over the National Highway to meet a T-junction where you turn left, signposted to "Rethymno 44". Then continue the directions from paragraph **A** on this page.

If heading from the National Highway:
Turn off for Agioi Pantes. Proceed 50m down to a crossroads where you turn left. Continue the directions from the next paragraph **A**.

A Proceed down to the bottom of this long straight road out of Agioi Pantes towards a left bend then bridge. Near this left bend, stop and look for a convenient parking place, maybe the narrow clear area under 2-3 large cypress trees, about 50m on the right before the bend, near a track turning off downhill, or at the clearing on the left immediately after the bridge.

This walk assumes you are starting from the 2-3 large cypress trees.

****

Crete Walks in the Apokoronas

With the 2-3 large cypress trees on your right proceed down the Old National Road for 25m to reach a wide track going ahead left downhill which you take, following the sign ΦΥΣΙΚΗ ΠΗΓΗ "ΑΣΠΡΟ ΝΕΡΟ" (Natural Well "White Water"). Proceed ahead over the brow and down the other side to reach another identical sign (as above) on the right indicating a track going ahead left bearing right downhill which you take into a cypress wood.

Just 20m beyond the first right bend, notice on the left the entrance to a small long tunnel running under the New National Highway. Continue along the main course of this track, passing the old Turkish water spring on the left, to reach a junction at a bend in the Old National Road where you turn ahead right.

Turkish Water Spring outside Agioi Pantes

Continue along the road to pass the Taverna Loutro and small church on the right. After a further 120m, follow the concrete track going steeply ahead left uphill.

Continue 600m along the main course of this track, ignoring any turnings off to the left or right, to reach a T-junction with a water standpipe opposite that goes up left over a brow and right downhill which you take. After just 5m, bear round to the left ignoring the track going ahead right downhill.

Continue on this track, ignoring a tarmac lane going back left bearing right over a brow, to soon reach a track off ahead left bearing right which you take.

Crete Walks in the Apokoronas

Continue 1200m along the main course of this track, passing a number of unnumbered water standpipes and a villa on the right with a miniature church just after it, and ignoring all the turnings off to the left and right.

Eventually you reach a peculiar junction with a water standpipe directly facing you. The main course of the track you are on makes a small joggle to the left to get round the water standpipe, but you take the track going back right in front of the water standpipe.

Continue on this track, round a series of bends, to meet a tarmac road going ahead left uphill and back right downhill. Take the track directly opposite going uphill to pass over a metal grating.

Follow this winding lane a short distance to a T-junction and turn right. Continue 100m further towards the large church of Fres which is already visible ahead.

In front of the church turn left (in the direction of the sign "Panayia of the Two Rocks"). Follow the road round to the right then left up to a T-junction, then turn left into Fres square where you can take some refreshments.

To visit one or two small but interesting churches at the top of Fres, departing from the square, see Walk 8 on page 63.

To continue the walk, retrace your steps out of the square with the arch behind you, then turn left. Continue directly ahead downhill, passing the sign "PERMONIA 2" on the left wall. Pass two staggered junctions, the first a road going right downhill, the second a road going back left uphill.

After a further 200m pass the "exiting Fres" sign on the right, then after a further 10m take the track off right downhill which has a wire fence on the left. Continue ahead through a left bend, passing the old stone threshing circle *(aloni)* over the wall on the right.

Continue downhill on the main course of this track, through a number of bends, to enter an olive grove as you bear round to the left. Proceed generally ahead through this olive grove for 200m, on a somewhat overgrown vehicular track, passing a small white concrete hut set back on the right.

Crete Walks in the Apokoronas

Eventually emerge onto a track appearing down left bearing right and ahead slightly right over a small brow which you take, passing a short section of stone wall on your right.

Continue ahead to a T-junction, with water standpipe 486 opposite, that goes right uphill and left downhill which you take.

Continue along this track, passing and ignoring two tracks going off to the left (the first going back left bearing right, followed after 4m by the second going ahead left uphill) as it bears round to the right.

Continue ahead for 550m on this track, passing water standpipes 482 and 481 both on the left, to reach a large walnut tree on the left. This is followed immediately by a track going back left uphill and 5m further on by a track going back right uphill, both of which you ignore to continue on the track ahead bearing left, generally in the same direction as before.

Continue 700m along the main course of this track as it twists and turns, ignoring all the turnings off to the left and right, passing on the right water standpipes 478 then 476 and a large pond. Eventually emerge onto the Old National Road at the small clearing under the 2-3 large cypress trees that was the starting point of the walk.

View on Walk

Crete Walks in the Apokoronas

WALK 2

ALIKAMBOS - Countryside to the South East

12 km – 3 hours

The Walk
This single-ended walk leaves Alikambos square along an ascending tarmac lane for 1.8km that winds its way out of the village. You eventually reach a gravel track that meanders its way for a further 4.2km through a wild landscape that is dominated by the White Mountains and which supports a number of sheep & goat farms. A memorial stone at the furthest end of the walk recalls a notable event near the end of the Turkish occupation of Crete. There are also great views of the landscapes below from near that high spot.

The Terrain
Less than a third of this walk is along one tarmac lane. The remainder is along one good gravel track that is easily passable. The walk to the end point is generally ascending, with the gradients of the first half of the walk being moderate and those of the second half to the end point being only slightly ascending or descending. The return is nearly all downhill.

The Start
Alikambos main square.

To get there from Vryses:
- Proceed out from Vryses following the road to Hora Sfakion,
- After crossing the river bridge in Vryses, proceed 750m to follow a sign on the right indicating "Αλικαμπος 6" (i.e. Alikambos 6) ahead,
- After a further 600m reach a T-junction with a major road and turn right,
- After 3.5km, at a sharp right-hand bend in the main road, turn down the lane off left signposted to "Alikambos 2",
- Follow that winding tarmac lane for 700m towards the "Church of the Koimesis" but on arrival turn round a 180° right-hand hairpin bend,
- Follow the tarmac lane, ignoring a fork ahead right downhill to continue round a left bend to enter Alikambos main square.

****

Crete Walks in the Apokoronas

Start with the Alikambos kafenion on your left and the war memorial with the two unexploded gun shells on your right. Proceed ahead along the tarmac lane bearing left over a slight brow.

Continue out of the village along the main course of this winding tarmac lane for 1800m, generally uphill, ignoring all turnings off to the left or right, noting these along your way:

- A fork back left, at a water standpipe and shrine on the left, with a sign ahead to "ΠΡΟΣ ΚΛΗΜΑ",
- A fork ahead left over a brow, at a right-hand bend in the tarmac lane, just after two steel gates on the left and before a sign ahead to "ΠΡΟΣ ΚΛΗΜΑ".

Eventually reach a point where the tarmac lane forks left uphill ahead just before a small square concrete pumping station, where a minor track goes off directly ahead. Take the tarmac fork left uphill which immediately changes to a gravel track.

Continue ahead for 4200m, generally uphill, on the main course of this winding track to its end, noting on your way:

- A small concrete livestock shed by the fence on the left,
- A track forking off right ahead that continues to climb up the hillside on the right,
- A long livestock shed down on the left in the distance,
- Two further livestock sheds on the right, possibly followed by some stock fences to go through.

Eventually the track ascends to a crossing of tracks that appear to go left uphill bearing right, right uphill bearing left, and slightly left ahead uphill which you take.

Continue for 200m to reach a clearing with a memorial stone on the right. This is the end point of this walk and a suitable place for a picnic.

> *The memorial stone commemorates the first meeting between Cretan revolutionaries and the then President (Manousos Koundourou) and General Secretary (Joseph Lekanis) of Crete, at that spot on 3rd September 1895, connected with the beginning of the liberation of Crete from Turkish rule.*

Crete Walks in the Apokoronas

There are excellent views of Georgioupolis beach and Kournas Lake to be seen from the top of the pile of stones at the far end of the clearing.

Please exercise due care and attention when climbing to the top as there are many loose stones and boulders, but the views are worth the effort if you can safely manage it.

The KΛHMA Memorial Stone

Retrace your steps back along the single-ended track for 4200m to arrive back at the small square concrete pumping station, now on your left.

Turn right onto the tarmac road, then retrace your steps back downhill for 1800m, ignoring all turnings off to the left and right, to arrive back in Alikambos square which was the starting point of the walk.

> *After the walk, stop off that the "Church of the Koimesis" on the way out of the village. It has some well preserved frescos inside that can be seen through a grill in the door. You will need a torch or the flash from a camera to properly see their details.*

WALK 3

APTERA – Ancient Greek, Roman and Turkish Ruins

6 km – 2 hours

The Walk
This mostly circular walk takes you through areas containing the well-preserved ruins of Greek, Roman and Turkish occupation, with the bonus of superb views of the White Mountains and Souda bay. The walk winds its way from the bottom of modern Aptera up to a section of wall that once surrounded the ancient Greek city of Aptera, before making its way further uphill to a Turkish fort that overlooks a second larger Turkish fort. The walk then comes back to visit the widespread ruins of ancient Roman Aptera before returning through some country tracks and lanes back to the starting point.

In 2009, the Roman site was open to the public, free of charge, from Tuesday to Sunday between 08.30 – 15.00 hrs (Monday closed).

The tavernas near the starting point, around the Aptera Taverna Triangle, are open throughout the summer but at least one (The Taverna Aptera) opens after 15.00 hrs during the winter months.

The Terrain
The first half of the walk to the top fort is along a tarmac road with moderately ascending or level gradients. The second half of the walk from the Roman ruins is on various good surfaces (tarmac, gravel, etc.) with generally downhill or level gradients.

The Start
From the National Highway follow the signs to Aptera. After a few bends pass a mini-market on the left just before a brow. Go over the brow to arrive at the Aptera Taverna Triangle (my name for that road junction) which you pass through bearing left. Immediately after it take the fork ahead right signposted to Stylos and Malaxa. Continue ahead for 80m and take the sharp fork ahead left uphill bearing right in front of the hotel on the left. You can park in one of the parking bays that are marked on the right side of this public road.

****

Crete Walks in the Apokoronas

To start this walk, proceed down out of the parking area and turn right towards the Aptera Taverna Triangle. After 80m take the tarmac lane going back right uphill that is directly opposite the Cretan Corner taverna on the left and is signposted to "Ancient Aptera".

Continue 1200m along the main course of this tarmac lane, passing the large hotel complex down on the right and ignoring any turnings off to the left or right, as it winds its way uphill. Pass a number of properties on both sides that make up part of modern Aptera.

Eventually reach a left bend in the road (1) in front of the reconstructed remains of a section of the old walls, dating from the 4th century BC, which once surrounded the Greek city of Aptera before its Roman occupation. The walls ran to a length of 3.5km round the hillside. There are a number of grave sites located in the areas outside these walls.

Follow the tarmac lane for 400m uphill bearing right to arrive at a junction (2) with a track going directly ahead signposted to "Ancient Aptera", and a fork ahead left signposted to "Koules Fortress" which you take. Proceed on the tarmac lane to its end, passing on the left a tall section of wall that is the remains of an ancient Greek temple.

Koules Fortress, Aptera

At the end of the road are the well-preserved walls of Koules Fortress. It was built around 1867 during the Turkish occupation of Crete (1669-1898) and is one of a number of fortresses built around the island by the Turks to help them control it during their occupation. Currently under restoration, it will eventually become a museum dedicated to the Turkish occupation, a gallery and centre for other cultural events.

Crete Walks in the Apokoronas

From this fortress there are splendid views all around, including that of a second Turkish fortress below called 'Izzedin'. This fort was more recently used as a prison for political dissidents between 1967-1974. More remains of the ancient wall that once surrounded the Greek city of Aptera are evident from this location, going around the hillside behind.

After visiting the features of the fort area, retrace your steps back along the tarmac road to the junction (2) above and turn back left onto the straight track that ends at a car parking area. The gate facing you on the left leads to the main site of the Roman ruins of Aptera. A second gate on the right leads to the Roman amphitheatre.

After visiting the features of the Roman site, with the entrance track facing you and the small kiosk on your left, proceed out of the car park and follow the track off ahead left bearing right between two low stone walls.

Inside the Large Roman Water Cistern, Aptera

Continue 400m along this ancient track, taking time to see the ruins of the "House with peristyle yard" along a track to the left, then passing the remains of two German machine gun installations from Second World War on the right.

Continue down a series of ancient steps to pass through the remains of one of the gates to the walled city of ancient Aptera, arriving back at the reconstructed remains of part of those walls (1).

Crete Walks in the Apokoronas

On reaching the tarmac road turn left downhill bearing right.

After 70m turn down a track going left downhill bearing left, soon to pass water standpipe 560 on the right. Proceed a further 200m to reach a track off right downhill which you take.

Roman Amphitheatre, Aptera

Continue 350m on the main course of this track to reach a T-junction with a track going up right and down left over a brow bearing left which you take.

Proceed 200m ahead to reach water standpipe 557 at a junction of tracks going left ahead uphill to a gate, right ahead downhill bearing left, and back right bearing left which you take.

Continue ahead 350m on the main course of this track as it winds its way up to some properties and a T-junction with a tarmac lane going down left and up right to a low brow which you take.

Continue 400m along the main course of this tarmac lane, going over two very small brows, and ignoring any turnings off to the left or right, to descend down to reach the large hotel on the right that was the starting point of the walk.

WALK 4

ARMENI – Orange Groves and River

6 km or 10 km – 2 hours or 3 hours

The Walk
This circular walk leaves Armeni to pass through numerous orange and olive groves before reaching a quiet picnic area alongside a flowing river. The return is through more citrus and olive groves, with a final easy section along a tarmac road back into Armeni. The walk can be extended to walk along sections of the river bank.

The Terrain
The walk is on tarmac lanes or good gravel tracks and lanes. If only doing the shorter walk through the orange and olive groves the gradient is almost flat all the way around. If you choose to also walk the additional section alongside the river bank there are some moderate gradients in the middle of the walk.

The Start
From Kalyves, take the road to Neo Chorio via Armeni. Pass through Armeni village to reach its large main church on the left, where you turn right into the lane opposite, from where this circular walk starts.

****

Start the walk in the lane directly opposite the large church in Armeni. With that large church behind you, proceed to a fork ahead right (1) and a fork ahead left which you take, passing water standpipe 88A on the left. After 160m reach a fork ahead right over a brow bearing left which you take. Pass water standpipe 83B on the left.

Continue ahead for 500m to reach a T-junction with a tarmac road going right and left with a track ahead bearing left directly opposite which you take. Reach after 350m a tarmac road going back right bearing right and ahead left uphill which you take.

Proceed 200m on this tarmac road to reach a junction with another tarmac road going back right and ahead left with a track directly opposite bearing right which you take, passing water standpipe 57 on the right near corner.

Crete Walks in the Apokoronas

Proceed 1300m along the main course of this winding track, passing in sequence:
- A fenced football pitch of Astoturf on the left (ignore the left turn immediately after it),
- A sharp left turn which you take, ignoring a minor track going off ahead,
- A riverbed on your left,
- Water standpipes 67 and then 67A on the right.

Eventually reach at a junction (2) with a tarmac road going back right over a little bridge, and ahead left bearing left which you take.

Continue 400m on the main course of this tarmac lane, passing water standpipe 70 on the right, to reach a bridge over a small river. This is an ideal place for a picnic.

Idyllic Scene at Suggested Picnic Area

Retrace your steps back to junction (2) above, passing water standpipe 70 now on the left, to reach the first left-hand bend where there is a deep water well below the square concrete feature on the left.

Continue along the tarmac lane, through the next two right-left bends and over the small bridge, to reach a sharp right bend with a minor track going back left which you take, passing water standpipe 69 in the left corner.

Continue 430m along the main course of this track, passing through a sharp left turn (with a water well on the right) then a right turn and water standpipe 68 on the left, to reach a junction of tracks going left bearing right, right bearing left, and ahead over a small bridge.

Option – To shorten the walk to 6km
Take the track going right bearing left. Continue 800m on the main course of this track to reach an old breeze block building on the right, just before a tarmac road going right and left which you take.

After 70m take the track going off slightly back right, just before a water standpipe on the left side.

Proceed along the main course of this track, passing through a right bend followed by a left bend, to reach water standpipe 144 opposite at a T-junction going left and right bearing left which you take.

Then continue with the shorter walk from paragraph **B** on Page 49.

Proceed ahead over the small bridge to a T-junction with another track going right towards water standpipe 85A, and left which you take. Pass water standpipe 85B on the right after which the river merges towards your left side.

Bamboo-lined Track Along River Bank

Continue ahead to a modern pumping station with a small picnic area (3), where you can take the follow interesting option:

Crete Walks in the Apokoronas

Option – To walk along a bamboo-lined track along the river bank
At the large square stone-clad plinth, cross over the river by the narrow green bridge and turn left. Walk the quiet bamboo-lined track for up to 300m along the river bank to its end at a ford, or as far as you wish to go. Return back to picnic area (3) at the pumping station.

To continue the walk, turn right uphill bearing left immediately after the pumping station. Continue ahead for 500m to eventually descend to a fenced enclosure directly ahead with a fork ahead left - *note the old donkey-operated chain well to the far left of this track* - and a fork ahead right which you take.

Donkey-operated Chain Well

Continue for 1800m on the main course of this long track, ignoring all turnings off to the left and right, to pass water standpipes 115, 114 and 113 all on the left, then water standpipes 127 and 131 on the right. Eventually you reach a junction of tarmac lanes going left uphill, ahead passing water standpipe 132 and a small shrine in the far left corner, and right uphill which you take immediately to turn left downhill keeping the long concrete wall on your left.

Continue 850m down to the bottom of this tarmac lane, passing water standpipes 176 and 177 on the right, to reach a junction of tracks going back left bearing left, back right, and ahead left which you take, keeping the concrete wall on your left.

Crete Walks in the Apokoronas

Continue 300m down to the end of this lane at a junction going ahead left over a very small bridge, and back right bearing left which you take.

Continue 1000m on the main course of this track, passing a large avocado grove on the left and water standpipes 143, 143A, 142, 142A all on the right. Reach a junction with a track going right uphill and left downhill which you take. Continue passed water standpipe 144 on the left.

B Continue 700m on the main course of this road, passing water standpipes 86, 87 and 88 on the left as you come back into Armeni.

Follow the road round to the right, passing a taverna set back on the left, to reach a fork right (1) which you ignore, water standpipe 88A opposite, and a fork ahead left to return back to the starting point of the walk.

One of the Armeni water springs is located behind the little white church of St John the Theologian, on your left as you arrive back at the starting point.

Large Church in Armeni

Crete Walks in the Apokoronas

WALK 5

DRAPANOS – Eastern Coastline

7 km – 2.5 hours

The Walk
This single-ended walk, on a clear day, provides extensive views across the bay to Georgioupolis beach, Rethymnon and beyond, with the high mountains of central Crete in the distance as a backdrop. There are good views of the coastline as you descend the eastern side of Drapanos Hill, with the best view being seen at the furthest point of the walk.

The Terrain
This walk is along a single tarmac lane that meanders round the hillside. There is a steady easy gradient downhill all the way, giving a steady easy ascent for the return.

The Start
From the Kokkino Horio direction proceed through Drapanos village, following the road round as it bears left and ignoring a right turn that is signposted to other villages. Proceed for 1.5km beyond the village, passing a small white church on the right before descending to reach a very short section of stone wall on the right with a green gate in the middle. You can park in the lay-by near the green gate.

Do not be tempted to follow the sign at the gate that points to a church down in the gorge below. This gorge is extremely dangerous and the church is at the bottom of the gorge.

****

From the lay-by at the green gate, proceed 2.5km downhill along the tarmac road as it meanders towards the bottom. Reach a livestock area on the left and a walled property on the right, with two stone arches in the front wall.

Continue a further 500m along the lane, passing a small communications mast and associated white hut on the right before bearing left to reach a right-hand hairpin bend with a deep gorge ahead going down to the sea.

Crete Walks in the Apokoronas

Continue a further 320m along the lane bearing right downhill to reach a left-hand hairpin bend with a small shrine in the corner. There are some nice views of the coastlines towards Ombrosgialos Bay and Georgioupolis beach from this bend – **BUT - Please do not get too close to the edge as it is loose and drops dangerously down to the sea a long way below.**

There are also some interesting formations and sections in the rocks on the right-hand side as you approach the left-hand hairpin bend.

View along walk towards Ombrosgialos Bay

Continue a further 240m, bearing left downhill, to reach the next right-hand hairpin bend which is the end point of this walk. This bend probably has the best views of the coastlines ahead to Vraskos Bay, and to the ends of the Drapanos and Akrotiri peninsulas. Along this section of lane you will be able to look down on the right to see it eventually terminating at a small military building.

It is probably prudent not to approach the military building any closer or to take any photographs of it.

To return, retrace your steps back up along the lane to the lay-by near the green gate.

Crete Walks in the Apokoronas

View towards Vraskos Bay

Rocks Formations at Hairpin Bend

WALK 6

EMBROSNEROS - Countryside to the North East

6 km – 2 hours

The Walk
This circular walk starts at the bottom of Embrosneros. It follows a quiet stone footpath up through a hidden wooded valley to an amphitheatre located in an area with numerous water springs coming out of the rocks around. The walk then passes two cave churches one above the other, the top one being large and beautiful, the lower one being much smaller. The walk then follows a loop of tracks and lanes around the countryside, returning to the top of Embrosneros to visit the ruins of the "Castle of Alidakis", the walk passes a large church in a picturesque setting and two more churches before the end of the walk.

The Terrain
Along a variety of surfaces that are easy to walk over, most being quiet tarmac roads or lanes. After leaving the tarmac lanes of Embrosneros there is 1km of gravel tracks and then 1km of tarmac roads that pass through the surrounding countryside before returning back to the top of Embrosneros. The walk then passes through the old narrow lanes of the village back down to the starting point. Gradients range from level to moderate, with some short steep sections.

The Start
Proceed out from Vryses following the road to Hora Sfakion. After crossing the river bridge in Vryses, proceed 750m and take a fork ahead right signposted to "Εμπροσνερος 5" (i.e. Embrosneros 5). Follow the main course of this road for 3km to arrive at the large fenced football pitch of Embrosneros on the right, just before entering the bottom of the village. Park in the lay-by on the left, opposite the football pitch.

****

With the football pitch on the right, proceed uphill ahead for 150m and go through the stone arch ahead at the right-hand hairpin bend. Continue 400m along the narrow stepped footpath, steep in places, as it winds its way uphill, passing through any stock fences you may encounter and ignoring a track back left uphill over a brow halfway along.

Crete Walks in the Apokoronas

Eventually reach the top at a modern amphitheatre with some surrounding buildings (still under construction in December 2009).

There are a number of natural water springs in this area, some running into stone troughs and some with more ornate carved stone surrounds. They may not all be flowing in dry weather.

Amphitheatre, Embrosneros

Walk round the top of the amphitheatre to find a water spring with an old carved stone surround. Then go back and climb the steps bearing right out from the amphitheatre onto the tarmac road.

Turn left bearing left to meet a junction with another tarmac going back right uphill (to a modern statue you can already see on the next bend) and ahead left bearing left which you take.

Continue 120m to a set of marble steps going back right uphill to the fabulous cave church which must be one of the best in Crete. After leaving the large cave church, walk round the path below it to reach another smaller cave church.

Retrace your steps back to the tarmac road and continue ahead. Ignore after 30m a lane going ahead downhill bearing left to continue uphill bearing right. After 40m follow the lane as it turns sharply ahead right uphill, to bear left then right. Ignore a tarmac lane going off back left downhill as you continue ahead over a brow bearing left downhill.

Crete Walks in the Apokoronas

Follow the main course of the lane for 130m to a junction going back left downhill bearing left and ahead right over a brow to bear left which you take, passing a small water standpipe on the right corner.

Follow the track for 240m to pass through the bottom of a dip bearing left, ignoring a track off back right uphill just after it. Continue ahead for 170m to pass over a brow with a turning off right to a small holding.

Continue a further 150m to pass through the bottom of a second dip bearing right, ignoring a track off ahead left downhill bearing left. Follow the main course of the track for 500m, climbing steeply for the last 50m after a sharp left bend, to reach a junction with a tarmac road going left downhill and right uphill which you take.

Follow the main course of this winding tarmac lane for 650m, ignoring any turnings off to the left or right, to reach two tracks going off left together as the lane you are on goes downhill bearing right then left.

Follow the main course of this winding tarmac lane for a further 260m, passing through a dip to reach a brow, passing a track going back right downhill bearing left, to reach just after it a junction with tarmac roads going left uphill bearing left, and ahead downhill bearing right which you take.

Follow the main course of the tarmac road for 500m, passing through a left-hand hairpin bend, to eventually reach a fork ahead right downhill into a square, and a fork ahead left uphill which you take. Proceed 70m along the lane to a bend going ahead left uphill which you ignore to take the narrow concrete footpath going directly ahead downhill.

Continue downhill ahead bearing right, down some steps, to arrive at a junction with a tarmac lane going ahead right downhill bearing left and left uphill which you take to arrive at the front of the Castle of Alidakis which is up on your left.

After visiting the castle ruins, ignore the first lane going left alongside the castle wall and take the next lane going ahead left over a brow.

Reach a junction with a lane going back right downhill bearing right and ahead left downhill bearing left which you take to pass between old properties No. 28 on the left and No. 26 on the right.

Crete Walks in the Apokoronas

Castle of Alidakis, Embrosneros

Continue downhill, passing the village primary school on the right, to reach a junction with a tarmac lane going ahead left downhill, and back right uphill over a brow bearing left which you take. Ignore the turning ahead right uphill immediately after the school playground.

Follow the main course of this lane downhill for 110m to reach an old square flat-topped building on the right, with a steel-barred window and rusty steel door, which is immediately before a narrow lane off right uphill which you take.

Reach a junction at the top of the lane going right uphill and left downhill which you take to enter a small square beyond which is a large picturesque church.

Proceed 30m ahead downhill passed the large church to reach a sharp hairpin bend (1) continuing back right downhill as a very narrow footpath which you take for 30m to arrive at another small church. **This footpath is slippery when wet - hold onto the railings on the left.**

Crete Walks in the Apokoronas

Retrace your steps back up to junction (1) above then turn right into a narrow concrete lane going uphill bearing left. Pass an old stone gateway at a ruined property No. 64 on the right.

Continue along this narrow lane to rejoin the main tarmac lane, now going ahead left uphill and back right downhill which you take.

Stepped Footpath at Beginning of Walk

After 110m reach a junction with a tarmac road going back right bearing right and ahead left soon to drop downhill bearing left. Cross over this road and take the narrow lane going ahead left downhill in front of a white wall.

Continue 200m down the lane, passing a church and cemetery down on the right, to reach a junction with a tarmac road going left uphill bearing right and right downhill bearing right which you take.

Continue downhill and through a left-hand hairpin bend to arrive back to the football pitch on the left which was the starting point of the walk.

Crete Walks in the Apokoronas

WALK 7

FRES - Countryside to the North East

9 km – 3 hours

The Walk
This walk, almost circular except for the first and last 800m, follows quiet country tracks for some distance before passing through an open area with a large number of dry-stone walls, then descending to the bottom of a tree-lined valley. The walk then ascends to a quiet tarmac road that is followed, for almost 2km, to pass two old ruined cottages and a small church, before joining more quiet country tracks to return to the start.

The Terrain
Along quiet country tracks, except for almost 2km along a quiet tarmac road. The surfaces of the country tracks, which are all vehicular, vary from concrete to grassy track, but most of the distance is along good gravel tracks. The gradients vary from mostly level to moderate, but the descent and ascent of the tree-lined valley are relatively steep.

The Start
Take the road from Agios Pantes towards Fres. Shortly after the "entering Fres", sign reach a sharp right-hand bend with a minor lane going off left signposted to "ΤΑΒΕΡΝΑ ΤΖΙΤΖΙΦΙΑ" which you take. After 200m pass a cemetery and church on the left. Park in the car parking area immediately after the cemetery.

****

Start with the cemetery behind you and the large cypress tree on the right. Proceed out of the parking area along the tarmac lane directly ahead.

Continue ahead for 370m, passing a small livestock area on the right, then a dry stone wall on the left with a concrete stripe running along it, to reach a small water standpipe on the left at a junction (1) with a track ahead left uphill over a brow which you take if not adding the following option.

Crete Walks in the Apokoronas

Option: To visit two small churches (adding 1.3km to the walk)

Continue ahead for 400m along the main course of the track. Reach the first church that is set back on the left in the ruins of a previous larger building. It has two millstones leaning up against its side wall.

Then continue a further 250m along the same track. Reach a track off left uphill bearing left which you ignore. Continue 30m further to reach a gap in a stone wall on the left, with a stock fence, that you go through to visit the second church that is visible 90m away on the left. It is surrounded by a number of walnut trees.

Retrace your steps back along the track to junction (1) and turn back right uphill over the brow.

Church, near Fres (First Optional Church)

Continue 450m along the track, going over the first small brow to reach the dip at a junction of tracks (2) going left into an olive grove, right downhill, and ahead uphill bearing right which you take.

Continue 600m along the track, going over a second brow, to reach the bottom of second dip at a junction with a tarmac road going ahead left uphill and back right downhill which you ignore.

Continue ahead 50m uphill to reach a junction with another track, going ahead left over brow bearing right, and back right downhill bearing right which you take.

Crete Walks in the Apokoronas

Continue 350m along the main course of this winding track, descending bearing left and ascending bearing right, to enter an extensive area with a large number of well-maintained dry stone walls, first passing a livestock area on the right.

After 140m, pass through a sharp left bend followed by a sharp right bend. Continue ahead, initially keeping a dry-stone wall on your right, to pass a small water standpipe on the right as the main track you are following bears left.

Continue 450m along the track as it winds its way through some long bends to reach a staggered junction of tracks, the first going back right downhill bearing right, the second going ahead bearing left, and the third that, after 20m, goes ahead right over a brow which you take.

Continue 280m along the main course of the track, passing a white property on the right and a track back right downhill immediately after it which you ignore, to reach a small church on the left.

> *This small church was still under construction in February 2010 with only the walls and roof being completed.*

Continue a further 180m along the track, passing a property up on the left, to reach a track off right downhill which you take. Continue on the main course of this track, passing after 300m a livestock area on the right at a left bend.

After a further 250m, pass thorough a tight right-hand hairpin bend and descend to a fork with a track going ahead right uphill bearing sharp right, and a track going ahead left downhill bearing right which you take.

Continue 230m along the main course of the new track to reach the bottom of the cypress tree-lined valley at a dried up riverbed.

Cross over the river bed and ignore the track back left following the riverbank to continue steeply uphill ahead bearing right.

After 230m pass through a left, then a right, hairpin bends. Reach after 60m, a junction (1) with a tarmac road going right downhill and left uphill. Here you have the following option.

Crete Walks in the Apokoronas

To shorten the walk by 1.5km, omitting Nippos village
Turn right downhill. Then continue the shorter walk from paragraph **B** on this page. Otherwise continue from below this photograph.

View along Track, near Nippos

Turn left uphill and continue 110m along the tarmac road to pass through a right-hand hairpin bend. Continue 250m further to reach, after passing the main church up on the left, the centre of Nippos at a T-junction with the main road going through the village.

Turn left, passing the war memorial on your right, to arrive at the well-respected local taverna 'ΤΑΒΕΡΝΑ ΙΠΠΟΚΟΡΩΝΙΟΝ' on your left which is the furthest point of the walk, and a very good place to take refreshments. When ready to return from Nippos, retrace your steps to 400m back down the tarmac road to the above junction (1).

B Continue downhill on the main course of the tarmac road for 550m, as it descends through a dip over a bridge bearing right, then ascends bearing left. Reach a sign "ΑΓΙΟΣ ΑΝΤΩΝΙΟΣ" on the right which points to the Church of Antonios that is just 50m below along the path.

Crete Walks in the Apokoronas

Continue a further 380m along the tarmac road, through a double right-hand bend, to pass an old ruined cottage up on the left, and a little further on water standpipe A2 and a track left uphill which you ignore.

Main Church, Nippos

Continue a further 540m along the tarmac road, through a left bend with another old ruined cottage in the near corner, passing water standpipe O.2 on the left, to reach a tarmac lane going back left uphill and water standpipe O.1 on the left immediately after it.

Continue a further 400m along the tarmac road, passing on the left a pair of wrought iron gates between two palm trees. Reach a right bend with a track off left bearing right which you take.

Continue 820m along the main course of this ascending track to reach a junction (2) with a track going right uphill bearing right, ahead into an olive grove, and left uphill bearing left which you take.

Continue 440m ahead, over a brow, to reach a junction (1) with a track going back left uphill and ahead right downhill which you take. Continue ahead for 370m to arrive back in the car parking area that was the starting point of the walk.

Crete Walks in the Apokoronas

WALK 8

FRES – Top Churches

2 km or 4 km – 1 hour or 2 hours

The Walk
This walk visits two small churches at the top end of Fres. The first church is known as the "Panayia of the Two Rocks" and is justifiably famous for its picturesque setting and well preserved frescos. The second church (optional) is much further up along the hillside above Fres and is well worth the difficult trek up to it for the expansive views of the countryside below.

The Terrain
Tarmac or concrete lanes lead up to the first church, the "Panayia of the Two Rocks". Then walk across a narrow stony and stepped concrete footpath to the beginning of the gravel track that climbs (optional) to and from the second church up on the hillside. The return routes from both churches follow the same tarmac lanes back to Fres square. The ascending gradients to the first church are moderate but with some quite steep sections towards the end rising up to the church. The gradients of the optional track up to the second church start off level and get progressively steeper as you get nearer the church. The returns from both churches are downhill nearly all the way back to the square.

The Start
Fres main square.

****

Start walking towards and through the arched exit from Fres square. Follow the lane ahead uphill as it bears slightly right after 40m. Continue 120m along this lane uphill and ignore the turning back right downhill bearing right as you bear round to the left.

Continue along the main course of this tarmac lane a further 350m as it winds its way uphill, ignoring any turnings off to the left or right.

Eventually reach a short narrow tarmac lane going ahead left steeply downhill in front of a sign pointing to the "Panayia of the Two Rocks" which you follow, ignoring the main tarmac lane as it bears right.

Crete Walks in the Apokoronas

At the bottom of the very short lane, meet another tarmac lane going ahead left downhill and back right uphill bearing left which you take to follow another sign pointing to the "Panayia of the Two Rocks".

Frescos in the Church "Panayia of the Two Rocks", Fres

Continue to follow this lane for 500m as it winds its way progressively more steeply uphill to the top where it levels off at the entrance to the church "Panayia of the Two Rocks" (Virgin Mary of the Two Rocks).

After visiting the church, walk across to the flat gravel bus parking area directly opposite to the right, possibly going through a stock fence.

Proceed out from the far end of this parking area, over a slight brow, to carefully follow a narrow footpath, rough in places, which continues ahead below a long string of light bulbs.

Eventually you pass over a series of concrete steps that lead up to a hairpin bend (1) in a concrete lane that marks the top end of Fres village. Here you have two options:

1. To return back to Fres square, thus shortening the walk to 2km.

    Turn ahead right downhill bearing right, then follow the directions from paragraph **C** on page 65.

Crete Walks in the Apokoronas

2. To visit the second church.

   Turn ahead left uphill over a brow. Continue to follow this lane for 1000m, which very soon becomes a track, as it climbs all the way up towards the small white church that you begin to see in front of you as you progress. The views from this church are well worth the considerable effort required to reach it.

   Retrace your steps back down the track to the concrete hairpin bend (1) and follow it round left downhill, then follow the directions from paragraph **C** on this page.

View Overlooking Fres from the Hillside Church

C Continue following the main course of this tarmac lane as it winds its way downhill for 1000m, ignoring any turnings off to the left or right. Ignore the lane going off ahead left downhill just after property No. 24 on the left as the lane bears round to the right. Continue downhill and through the arched entry into Fres square which was the starting point of the walk.

Crete Walks in the Apokoronas

WALK 9

GAVALAHORI - DOULIANA

8 km – 3 hours

The Walk
This 'figure of eight' walk leaves Gavalohori square for the village of Douliana over a number of quiet tracks and lanes through the countryside. After 5.5km of walking you arrive at the village of Douliana with its traditional kafenion. The return route takes you down an old donkey track and passed an interesting cave church, then along more quiet tracks and lanes back to Gavalohori square.

The Terrain
The walk is mostly on easy-going quiet country tracks, apart from one 350m section of tarmac road after 2.5km that joins two tracks but this is not a main road. There is also one section of old donkey track going steeply downhill with stones that are easy to walk over with due care. This walk has quite a number of gradients that are mostly moderate but there are a couple of short steep sections.

The Start
Gavalohori main square.

****

With the war memorial on your left, leave Gavalohori main square by the narrow lane on the right, then after 5m reach a sign pointing to the "MUSEUM" down a lane on the right which you take.

Continue ahead on the main course of this narrow winding lane, passing a small white monument on the right, followed by a narrow lane on the right that has a sign to the "MUSEUM".

The folklore museum is just 15m up the lane on the left.

In 2009 it was open at the following times:

Monday to Saturday: 09.00 -19.00
Sunday: 11.00 - 18.00
Entrance: €2 in 2008 (children under 12 are free).

Crete Walks in the Apokoronas

Continue ahead to pass a large church on the right, soon to go uphill bearing left, ignoring a concrete track going off slightly ahead right uphill (1).

Follow this tarmac road round to the right, passing a large school building and play area on the right, to bear left downhill. Reach a junction with a road going back left uphill and ahead right downhill bearing left which you follow, to take after 80m the track going off ahead right downhill.

Follow the main course of this track downhill, passing an unusual stone shrine on the right, then a fork back left uphill, as the track bears right downhill.

Stone Wall and Shrine

Continue to the bottom of the hill (2). Ignore a turning off back right uphill to ascend through a small left-right joggle up the hill ahead and over a brow.

Pass through another dip, at a junction of tracks (3) with a concrete building on the right, to continue on the main track uphill ahead bearing right. Continue for 700m along the main course of this track, to reach a brow with a white shrine on the right, dated 1961, just before a track off ahead right uphill which you ignore to continue downhill on the main track.

Crete Walks in the Apokoronas

Continue 100m down the hill to reach a fork ahead right downhill which you take to pass a white villa a short distance further along on the left which you can already see.

Continue 500m further along the main course of this track, which changes to become a tarmac road, as it winds its way downhill to reach water standpipe 239A on the left, just **after** a track off back left steeply uphill which you now go back and take.

Continue 400m on the main course of this track to meet another track going off ahead left uphill which you ignore, as you continue ahead right downhill to go between two wire fences as the track bears round to the left.

Continue 300m to a junction with another track, at a small clearing, that goes ahead right downhill and back left uphill which you take. After only 30m follow the main course of the track as it forks ahead right uphill, ignoring the minor fork slightly ahead left uphill over a brow.

Proceed 600m along the main course of this track, as it goes over a brow and down passed an avocado grove on the right, to meet another track going back right down and ahead left uphill which you take.

Continue uphill for 700m, ignoring the fork ahead left uphill as you bear right, and passing a shrine on the right dated 28/10/93, to reach the restored washing wells of Douliana village on the left.

> *Note the holes in the stones projecting outwards at the front that were used in days gone by to tie up the donkeys.*

Continue for 430m along the main course of the winding lane as it ascends alongside the right-hand edge of Douliana village, passing on the left a tall stone wall and water standpipe 11 on the left, to reach the Apartments Theano also on the left.

Take the narrow lane ahead left uphill bearing left immediately after the Apartments Theano.

Follow the narrow lane to its end at a small square (4), with a memorial stone on the left, where you can now take the following option, or else skip to the next main paragraph after it.

Crete Walks in the Apokoronas

Option: To see more of the village and visit the Taverna Douliana
Turn left and go downhill bearing left to enter another small square with a miniature church on the left. Continue into an area with some magnificent new properties. To visit the Taverna Douliana, take the first left turn after the miniature church and proceed to its end. Then retrace your steps back to the small square (4) above and continue with the next paragraph below.

From the small square (4), with the memorial stone behind you, proceed 50m down the lane ahead right bearing left to reach another larger square with a charming traditional Greek kafenion on the left.

To continue the walk, with the kafenion on your left, retrace your steps back for 40m along the lane and turn right into a narrow lane going steeply downhill.

Continue down the narrow lane, ignoring a minor track off ahead left in front of a water standpipe, as it becomes a narrow donkey track of large stones that winds its way downhill in front of you.

Ignore a very minor track off directly ahead where the donkey track turns sharply right downhill which you follow (there are some plastic water pipes running along the bottom of the left wall at this point).

Continue down to the bottom of the donkey track, then turn left onto another narrow track. Continue along the track to a tall flat wall on the right with a door leading to the small cave church of St John.

> *In many such small churches there may be evidence of human skeletons. These will be the remains of persons whose bones have had to be removed from their first marble grave above ground to make room for the body of the next deceased person.*
>
> *This is the normal practice in Greece where owing to the rocky ground it is not possible to inter bodies below ground, so the families 'rent' a marble grave above ground for about 3-4 years after which their bones have to be removed by the family and deposited elsewhere.*

After leaving the church, continue your progress along the track, passing over some natural rock outcrops as you cross over a dry riverbed.

Crete Walks in the Apokoronas

Cave Church of St. John, Douliana

Continue ahead, with the riverbed on now your left, to again reach the junction of tracks (3) now appearing left uphill, ahead slightly right downhill with the concrete building on its left side, and right uphill bearing left over a brow which you take.

Continue 130m over a brow to the bottom of the next dip (2) and take the fork left ahead uphill. Follow the main course of this track for 900m to its end, passing on the way two villas on the right separated by a shared carport, to arrive at a tarmac road (1) appearing right back uphill and left ahead downhill which you take.

Retrace your steps 300m down along the tarmac road towards Gavalohori, passing the large church on the left and continuing ahead through the narrow lane to arrive at a T-junction where you turn left to enter the main square which was the starting point of the walk.

WALK 10

GEORGIOUPOLIS – Beach Walk

6 km – 2 hours

The Walk
This single-ended walk takes in the village of Georgioupolis and its 4km of superb beach, a long and wide stretch of golden sand. The walk can be started from the busy Georgioupolis end, and then heading out along the shoreline to reach a small stream coming down from the White Mountains, or started from that stream and heading out along the shoreline towards busy Georgioupolis.

Georgioupolis has much to see, with its small harbour, church of St. Nicholas on a promontory, model of the Acropolis, tavernas, shops and many other facilities.

The beach has a number of low rise hotels built along it that are towards the Georgioupolis end, but these are respectfully set back from the shoreline as to not adversely affect the enjoyment of this stroll.

The Terrain
Flat all the way. There is a short section of promenade in Georgioupolis and the rest is along the sandy shoreline.

Georgioupolis Beach towards Georgioupolis

Crete Walks in the Apokoronas

The Two Starts
The walk can be started from either end depending on how you want the walk to be.

1. If starting from the harbour at Georgioupolis, the walk starts and ends along the promenade with the sandy beach forming the main part of the walk (use Walk Sequence 1 below).

2. If starting from the far end of the beach, the walk makes its way along the beach to the promenade and into Georgioupolis with all its facilities. It then returns back along the promenade and the beach to the starting point (use Walk Sequence 2 below).

   Walk Sequence 1 - Georgioupolis to Beach: A - C - D.
   Walk Sequence 2 - Beach to Georgioupolis: B - D - C.

   ****

A) Park in the large car park between Georgioupolis harbour and the sea.

B) Assuming you are going to drive to the starting point from Georgioupolis main square:

   - Proceed out of Georgioupolis main square towards the National Highway,
   - After 60m take the ahead left turn signposted "Rethymno 32 Kournas 8",
   - Proceed ahead over the brow, then bear right to cross over the National Highway,
   - Proceed to the end of the straight section of road, then bear left and immediately right to follow the road signposted to the Pilot Beach Resort that runs in front of and parallel to the National Highway – **DO NOT JOIN THE NATIONAL HIGHWAY**.
   - Proceed 2km along the road and 60m BEFORE a narrow bridge ahead, turn left through the concrete tunnel running under the National Highway,
   - Exit the tunnel, turn left and then immediately right to enter a car parking area where you park.

   There is what looks like a mound of stones piled up on your left which is actually a Second World War bomb shelter.

C) With the sea in front of you, walk to the end of the promenade, turn right and follow it to its end.

Pass the sign for the 'Perastikos Café-Restaurant' and immediately turn right to cross a narrow footbridge, noting the bubbling sand in the water to the near left end of the bridge.

Pass up the left side of the taverna building. Continue 50m ahead on the gravel track to a T-junction going ahead right and back left bearing right which you take, following it round left to its end on the beach, passing a small palm tree plantation on your right.

Turn right and walk along the beach, crossing over any very narrow streamlets you find that are easy to hop across. Eventually you will come to a group of large stones strewn the sand just ahead of a shallow stream coming down from Kournas lake.

There is what looks like a mound of stones piled up on your right which is actually a Second World War bomb shelter.

Return by following Section D.

D) With the bomb shelter on your left, walk along the beach towards Georgioupolis, crossing over any very narrow streamlets you find that are easy to hop across.

When almost reaching the end of the beach, after all the large hotels, look out for the brown wooden La Palma Beach Bar on the left and exit the beach by a gravel track immediately after it.

Continue on the track ahead bearing right to reach a junction off back right downhill that is signposted to the 'Perastikos Beach Restaurant' which you take.

Follow the track a short distance to step down onto and cross a narrow footbridge immediately ahead of you, noting the bubbling sand in the water to the far right end of the bridge.

Turn left and walk along the beach to eventually reach the promenade which you follow to its end at the car park near Georgioupolis harbour.

Crete Walks in the Apokoronas

If you started from the beach end (Walk Sequence 2) this is the furthest point. You are now free to wander around Georgioupolis.

Do not miss the opportunity to visit the:

- The Church of St. Nicholas on the rocky promontory,
- The amazing model of the Acropolis at the taverna along the far end of the beach.

Return by following Section C.

Georgioupolis Beach towards Rethymnon

Model of the Acropolis, Georgioupolis

WALK 11

KAINA - Countryside to the South East

5 km – 1.5 hours

The Walk
This triangular walk leaves the outskirts of Kaina village. The first side follows a quiet track almost parallel with the road to Vamos although you would hardly realise it. The second side follows a quiet tarmac lane with clear views of the White Mountains. The third side follows more quiet tracks and lanes back to Kaina. At the end of the walk there is an option to wander through some of the lanes of this old village which seems to have been ignored by tourist literature, maybe deliberately so that it can retain its anonymity.

The Terrain
The first side of the triangle (2km) has good gravel tracks or tarmac/concrete surfaces with generally ascending gradients and some short steep sections.

The second side (1km) is a tarmac lane descending all the way. The third side (2km) has good gravel tracks or tarmac/concrete surfaces with sections of ascending and descending gradients.

The additional walk through the village is ascending to the top of the village and descending back to the starting point. Most gradients are moderate with a few short steeper sections.

The Start

If heading from Vamos towards Kaina:

- Proceed passed the "exiting Vamos" sign on the right,
- Then go over a brow,
- Continue ahead downhill for some distance on this winding road to reach the bottom at a sweeping left-hand bend just before climbing up into the village,
- At the bottom of this dip there is a wide lay-by on the right-hand side where you can park.

Crete Walks in the Apokoronas

If heading from Agioi Pantes towards Kaina:

- Proceed through the village of Kaina, over a brow bearing left,
- Reach a sweeping right-hand bend at the bottom of a hill after the last houses,
- At the bottom of this dip there is a wide lay-by on the left-hand side where you can park.

****

With the lay-by on your right proceed up the hill towards the village and take the first turning left ahead downhill after the first property.

Continue down the hill and up the other side to a brow, ignoring a back right downhill turning off just before it and passing water standpipe A439 on the right just after it.

Continue ahead on the main course of this winding track as it meanders generally uphill for some distance, passing the dog kennels on the right where there may be a lot of barking heard.

> *These are the lucky dogs that are being properly looked after by a caring English person, a situation that unfortunately many Cretan dogs do not enjoy.*

Continue ahead to reach a delightful little church (1889), known locally as "Ιεροσ Ναοσ το Γενεθεολιον τησ θεοτοκου" (Holy Temple of the Mother of God) that is set in its own well-tended grounds.

Follow the track to the left of the church and continue ahead for 350m, passing water standpipe 424 on the right.

Eventually reach a junction with water standpipe 423 opposite, a track off ahead left, a tarmac road going left, and a tarmac road going back right downhill which you take.

Continue for 1km down the tarmac road, passing along the way:

- Water standpipes 425 and 426 on the right,
- A small church on the right,
- Water standpipe 427 on the left.

Eventually reach a number of properties on the left as the road bears round uphill to the right. Here you ignore a turning off to the left to continue ahead bearing right, passing on the left after 20m an old stone arch for property No. 10.

Stone Arch outside No. 10

Continue on this tarmac lane, over the brow to pass properties on the right then left, to reach water standpipes 436 and 435 on the right, and 434 on the right as you bear round to the left.

Continue downhill to bear right, ignoring the track off ahead and passing water standpipe 437 on the left. Continue down to the bottom of the hill, passing water standpipe 442 on the left before passing a small round white storage building on the right.

Continue uphill to pass water standpipe 441 on the left over a brow. Continue downhill then uphill, bearing right at water standpipe 440 on the right, noting the stone wall immediately facing which has an old tree trunk embedded into it.

Continue uphill, passing water standpipe 439 on the left as you go over yet another brow. Proceed to the bottom of the hill bearing right then left, ignoring the fork going off back right uphill at the bottom of the dip.

Crete Walks in the Apokoronas

Continue uphill for 140m to reach a junction with a lane going left downhill and ahead right uphill bearing right which you take, reaching after 40m the main road through the village.

At this point you could decide to add the option below for a short walk to the top of the old village of Kaina, or else conclude the walk with the next paragraph.

Turn right downhill and follow the main road out of the village for 150m to arrive back at the lay-by on the left which was the starting point of the walk.

Option: A Walk through Kaina Village (Additional)
Cross over the main road, keeping the large tree on your right. Follow the lane ahead, passing the side of the small kafenion on your left and the main church followed by the disused school house on your right.

Continue uphill, ignoring a lane going off back right with a tree in the near corner, to reach a small square with a small white concrete block in the centre where you continue uphill bearing left.

Continue to a fork ahead left over a brow and a fork ahead right which you take to pass another church on the left. Continue along the lane as far as you wish to go, passing the last properties in the village before ascending out into the countryside.

Retrace you steps back down the hill, bearing right through the square with the small white concrete block in the centre, to reach the fork left ahead with the small tree facing which you take. Turn down the first narrow lane off right immediately after the white wall.

Continue down this lane, passing the old school house and playing ground on the right, to reach the main road through the village. Turn left to return to the lay-by which was the starting point of the walk

WALK 12

KALAMITSI ALEXANDROU & KALAMITSI AMYGDALI

3.5 km or 7 km – 1.5 hours or 2.5 hours

The Walk
This circular walk starts/ends in the centre of Kalamitsi Alexandrou. It leaves the village to descend a pleasant gorge before climbing steeply for 350m to connect with another at a higher level.

The walk then follows that track round the hillside, with nice views towards Georgioupolis and down to the valley below, before descending to the bottom of a second gorge.

Halfway up the second gorge there is the interesting little church of St. Eleusa and a shaded picnic area. At the top of the second gorge, in the sister village of Kalamitsi Amygdali, there is a kafenion. The route back to Kalamitsi Alexandrou is along a series of quiet country tracks and lanes.

The Terrain
A variety of surfaces ranging from smooth tarmac to gravel tracks, and a variety of gradients ranging from flat to moderate. The first gorge has a moderate gradient all the way down, and the second gorge has a moderate gradient all the way up. There is one steep track ascending for 350m which is narrow and potentially muddy in wet weather.

The Start
Kalamitsi Alexandrou main square.

Driving along the Vamos to Georgioupolis road, pass the 'entering Kalamitsi Alexandrou' sign and the small blue/white church on the left. Where the road then bears round sharp left, ignore the fork back right and take the right ahead turning signposted to 'Vryses 3'. Proceed along this narrow winding lane to enter the village square with its old well on an island in the centre. Either park somewhere convenient in the village square, or continue through the village to find a very suitable parking area just after the last property on the left under a row of cypress trees.

****

Crete Walks in the Apokoronas

Start the walk with the memorial bust on the left and the old blue well on the right. Proceed 40m to a fork ahead right and fork ahead left bearing left which you take.

Continue to follow this lane for 300m, passing a few more properties and going down out of the village to the bottom of a dip where you turn left onto a track going ahead downhill.

Continue descending this track through the small gorge for 1100m to the bottom, passing a small farmstead on the right halfway down, to reach a fork ahead left uphill and a fork ahead right downhill bearing left. At this point turn around, go back 10m and take the track now appearing ahead right steeply uphill.

Ascend this steep track for 350m to meet another track going ahead left uphill and back right downhill where you now have the following option.

To shorten the walk to 3.5km, omitting Kalamitsi Amygdali village
Turn left uphill and follow the track round bearing right, to meet after 170m a track going back left downhill which you take. Then continue the shorter walk from paragraph **D** on page 82.

To continue on the full walk, take the back right downhill track and follow its main course for 1.3km as it meanders round the hillside, eventually descending into a dip to meet a junction with a lane going down right and up left which you take to commence your climb up the second gorge.

Proceed up the gorge for 400m to a section where the track widens, with a stone wall ahead of you and a large plane tree on the right. Take the narrow lane going off right over a few steps to reach the small church of St. Eleusa the other side of a short tunnel formed by a huge fallen rock.

After visiting the church, return to the main tarmac lane, turn right and continue up the gorge for 100m to arrive at a picnic area on the left.

> *Below the covered picnic table is a water trough where in days gone by the women from Kalamitsi Amygdali would come down to do their washing.*

Crete Walks in the Apokoronas

Follow the main course of the lane up the gorge for 700m, passing water standpipe 27 on the right and water standpipe 26 on the left, to emerge at a junction on a bend of the Vamos to Georgioupolis road that bypasses the village. Turn left downhill to pass the war memorial on the left and 70m further on to reach a kafenion on the right.

Church of St. Eleusa, Kalamitsi Amygdali Gorge

To continue the walk from the kafenion, cross over the road slightly left and follow the lane that runs alongside the white property that has red and green marine navigation lights on the front wall. Continue ahead uphill through the lane for 250m to reach a junction with the road sweeping round the front of the main church facing you. Follow the road round to the left, passing the Villa Dimitris on the left.

After 80m, pass through the left-right joggle downhill to reach a sharp left corner with a narrow lane going off directly ahead which you take. After 20m turn right, noting a plaque in the corner wall saying "Crete-Contact", to pass the church/cemetery on the left. After the church, reach a junction with a lane going right and down left which you take.

Continue on the main course of this track for 700m as it winds its way to the bottom of a dip and up again to reach a junction of tracks going left uphill, ahead right downhill into an olive grove, and right uphill bearing left over brow which you take, keeping a stone wall on the left and a wire fence on the right.

Crete Walks in the Apokoronas

Continue on this track ahead as it winds its way over a brow to bear right downhill to a sharp left bend, 10m after which you take the track off ahead right downhill.

D Continue ahead to pass a large plastic greenhouse on the right and water standpipe 42 on the left. After a further 40m follow the main route of the track as it bends sharp right, keeping the wire fence on your right and ignoring a minor track going ahead left into and olive grove.

Countryside on this Walk

Continue on the main course of this track, ignoring any turnings off to the left or right, as it winds its way for 120m through the olive grove to ascend onto another track going back left downhill and ahead right uphill which you take.

Continue on the main course of this track for 350m, through sharp right and left bends, to emerge up onto a tarmac lane going right downhill and left uphill over a brow which you take. Continue 200m ahead on this tarmac lane to a junction with another tarmac lane going ahead left uphill bearing right over a brow and ahead right downhill bearing right which you take to pass property No. 33 on the right.

Continue on this tarmac lane as it bears round to the left before rising up to a junction with the main road into Kalamitsi Alexandrou, going ahead right bearing right and directly ahead bearing right uphill which you take. Continue on this tarmac lane ahead as it enters the main square which was the starting point of the walk.

WALK 13

KOKKINO HORIO – North East

8 km – 2.5 hours

The Walk
This walk meanders through the old village on Kokkino Horio, used for many of the scenes in the 1964 film "Zorba The Greek", before following tarmac lanes down to a small smugglers cove. The walk continues along a quiet track to a large sea cave before retracing steps back to the tarmac road and continuing to a lighthouse. The walk returns to complete a small loop around the village of Kokkino Horio.

The Terrain
This walk has easy tracks and quiet tarmac roads and lanes around much of its route. There are some steep gradients in places.

The Start
From Plaka, proceed through Kambia towards Kokkino Horio. As you enter Kokkino Horio the road forks ahead right and ahead left which you take. Pass the large church on the right to enter a square with a basketball court on the left where there is free parking space.

Beware of the 'No Parking' signs on one side of the basketball court.

****

From the basketball court, with the church on your right, walk down the lane into the old village of Kokkino Horio. Pass a mini-market on the left. Follow the lane through a left downhill bend, ignoring the lane coming down from the right at this point.

Continue down the lane bearing right to a small square. Ignore the track directly ahead and take the narrow lane going ahead right to follow the sign for "ΡΟΥΜΑΤΣΑΛΙ" (a district within the village).

Continue along the main course of this lane as it bears right then left, ignoring lanes off to the left and right as you pass a number of interesting old stone houses on either side - on a left bend there is low stone wall in front of you that you can look over to see more of the old stone houses and courtyards.

Crete Walks in the Apokoronas

Continue down the lane, passing a pair of green gates on the left, to reach a "STOP" sign before a tarmac road going back right and directly ahead which you take. Follow the road for 80m and bear left downhill following the sign to "ΑΒΛΟΧΙΑ".

Continue down the road for 650m to the bottom, turning round a sharp left bend just ahead of the junction (1) with a tarmac road going ahead left and back right which you take, following the signpost to "ΦΑΡΟΣ 2".

Continue walking downhill on this tarmac lane for 900m to reach a yellow sign for "ΚΟΥΤΑΛΑΣ" (2) at a turning left downhill bearing right which you take. Follow the track down 250m towards a cove that starts opening up in front of you near a white villa on the right.

Opposite the gates of the villa there is a fork ahead left downhill that leads down to the once isolated smugglers cove.

Smugglers Cove, Kokkino Horio

Retrace your steps back to the top track and turn left to continue in the same direction as before.

Crete Walks in the Apokoronas

Follow the main course of the track 400m to its end, ignoring a right turn towards two villas, then passing between two steel gate posts with maybe a stock fence across them, and turning sharp right at two metal gates ahead, to eventually reach a set of stone steps going down to a large sea cave.

Do not attempt to cross over into the cave if the water is rough or you do not have suitable footware as the rocks are slippery when wet.

Retrace your steps back to the junction (2) above with the yellow sign for "ΚΟΥΤΑΛΑΣ". Turn left and follow the road, passing a pink property on the right after 400m, to see a tall military communications aerial in view on the right in the grounds of a military base.

Do not take photographs in this area until returning back to the pink property at point (3) below. Just enjoy the nice views.

Sea Cave, Kokkino Horio

Continue 700m along the lane ahead, passing the fenced military base on the right and taking the fork ahead left, to reach a right bend where there are some steps on the left going down to the lighthouse which is the furthest point of the walk.

Crete Walks in the Apokoronas

Retrace your steps all the way back passed the pink property (3), now on you left.

You can now resume taking photographs.

Coastline near Sea Cave, Kokkino Horio

Continue ahead on the tarmac road to reach the "ΦΑΡΟΣ 2" sign (1) where you ignore the turning back left uphill that you came down earlier to continue ahead.

Follow the main course of this road for 650m as it bends to the left then right, passing a series of modern villas either side, to eventually reach a left turn going steeply uphill bearing left which you take.

Continue along the main course of this steeply ascending and winding lane for 400m to reach a T-junction with another lane going ahead left and back right which you take, then bear right after the first property on the right to pass the mini-market on the right.

Continue ahead on the main course of this lane, soon to reach the basketball court that was the starting point of the walk.

WALK 14

MELIDONI – Foothills of the White Mountains

17 km – 5 hours

The Walk
This single-ended walk leaves Melidoni, one of the highest villages in the foothills of the White Mountains, to follow a number of quiet tracks that climb much higher up into the foothills of the White Mountains to an altitude of just over 1000m above sea level.

As you progress up through the many hairpin bends the views change to become more spectacular. The walk reaches a small plateau with some old disused shepherd's buildings that makes the perfect place to stop for a picnic where you can enjoy some of the most spectacular views on Crete. You might spot an eagle soaring by on a thermal.

The walk gets progressively more difficult the higher up you get. If you decide to walk only so far before turning back, you will still be able to enjoy some superb views.

The Terrain
Walking is initially over tarmac or concrete, then mostly on gravel lanes or tracks with some of these being rough in places. The gradients uphill and downhill range from level to moderate initially, increasing from moderate to steep the higher up you get.

The full walk is not easy and you should be fit before attempting it.

The Start
Drive through Permonia towards Melidoni village. On passing the 'entering Melidoni' sign and the war memorial on the right, reach the small square with a telephone booth on the left, then take the first left turn immediately after. Proceed to the end of that short straight road, do a U-turn at the end and park anywhere convenient in that area. Walk back to the large rectangular concrete tank (a water reservoir) at the top end of that road.

****

Crete Walks in the Apokoronas

Start with the concrete reservoir behind you and the two blue road signs in front on you. Turn left and follow the tarmac lane signed to "ΠΡΟΦ. ΗΛΙΑΣ". Proceed along the main course of this tarmac lane, ignoring a minor track going off ahead right uphill bearing right as you pass over a brow near an unmarked water standpipe on the right.

Continue ahead on the main course of the winding lane for 1000m to reach a junction of tracks (1) going left downhill, ahead over a brow bearing right, and right bearing left signed to "ΑΓΙΟ ΠΝΕΥΜΑ" which you take.

As you proceed from this point up to the highest point of the walk, note the changing scenery and the amazing views.

Continue ahead, ignoring after 50m a minor gravel track going ahead right uphill bearing right, to instead follow the direction of the sign to "ΠΡΟΦ ΗΛΙΑΣ".

Continue ahead for 1.3km on this winding track, passing along the way:

- A small concrete hut on the right,
- A small vehicular turning area on the left,
- An old metal swing barrier which you pass through,
- A few livestock buildings on the left,

to eventually reach a fork ahead left downhill bearing left into a dip which you take, thus ignoring the main track as it proceeds ahead bearing left in the direction of the sign "ΑΓΙΟ ΠΝΕΥΜΑ".

Proceed on the track ahead bearing left through a small valley containing a number of livestock buildings, shepherds huts and cultivated areas.

As you leave this valley you see ahead of you the daunting prospect of the grey gravel track you are about to climb as it snakes its way up the hillside.

Proceed 1.5km to the top of this visible track to reach a left bend where the track continues 130m to a rock cutting immediately before a right bend.

Crete Walks in the Apokoronas

As you proceed from this point up to the highest point of the walk, note the changing geology and unusual rock formations.

One of the Views on this Walk

Continue to ascend this single-ended track for 400m, passing through a right then left hairpin bend, to reach at a height level with the top of the conical hill on the left a 90° left bend with an exposed vertical rock face on the right showing unusual rock formations.

After a further 700m, reach a small plateau at a left hairpin bend with a long livestock building to the right in amongst the cypress trees and a fenced enclosure facing.

After a further 750m, reach a right bend over a brow onto a small plateau (2) containing an old derelict shepherds cottage and other stone structures that are now used for livestock.

Walk across the plateau and after a further 300m, pass through a final pair of right-left hairpin bends, to reach a long stone-walled, stone-roofed cottage and some fenced enclosures. This is the end point of the walk.

Crete Walks in the Apokoronas

Stone Hut

Retrace your steps back down to the plateau with the old derelict shepherds cottage. Have a well-earned rest and picnic to enjoy the views of the countryside below and for some considerable distance beyond.

When ready to return back to Melidoni, retrace your steps back down the track, passing through the valley with the cultivated area and livestock buildings, to rejoin the main track at the junction with the sign "ΑΓΙΟ ΠΝΕΥΜΑ" that goes back left uphill and ahead right which you take.

Continue to descend back to the junction of tracks (1) where you now turn left downhill.

Continue for 1.7km on the main course of this lane, ignoring any turnings off to the left or right, until you eventually reach the enclosed concrete rectangle at the top of Melidoni, where you turn right to return to the starting point of the walk.

WALK 15

MOURI (near KOURNAS LAKE) - Countryside to the East

5 km – 1.5 hours

The Walk
This circular walk starts/ends on a quiet road leading up to the small village of Mouri, near the freshwater Kournas Lake. There is easy parking even on busy weekends and bank holidays. The walk goes through Mouri village to fork off into the quiet countryside that is completely hidden from the lake.

Although this walk is near Kournas Lake it is not a feature of it. However the lake and its facilities can be easily visited afterwards.

The Terrain
Mostly gravel tracks and lanes. There are two short sections of quiet tarmac road. The first half of the walk has varying gradients with one particularly long steep climb. After that the walk follows a ridge of either level or gentle downhill gradients for 1.5km before reaching a level section. A last short moderate climb and descent takes you back to the starting point.

The Start
Taking the road out of Georgioupolis, follow the signs for Kournas or Kournas Lake. Before you get to the lake, pass a tall grey property on the left with a curved front wall, followed by a long white wall on the right. Slow down immediately after the wall ready to turn back left into an almost concealed left turn. Continue along this winding road, over the first brow with water standpipe 71 on the left, then to the top of the second brow, with water standpipe 63 on the left, where you turn right. Proceed along this road to a narrow verge on the right side where you can park.

****

Start the walk going uphill towards Mouri village. Reach a fork (1) ahead right bearing left and fork ahead left bearing right which you take. Continue 370m on the main course of this tarmac road through the village to reach water standpipe 56 on the left at a fork ahead left downhill which you take.

Crete Walks in the Apokoronas

Continue on this track downhill, passing water standpipe 55 on the left, to reach a brow with water standpipe 53 on the right and a fork back right which you ignore.

Continue over the brow to reach a junction with a track going left bearing left and right bearing right which you take to pass water standpipe 47 on the left.

Climb the hill ahead for 500m, passing along the way:
- A track going off right ahead downhill,
- A track going back left uphill bearing right,
- A wall of very large stones on the left,

to eventually reach a fork right ahead uphill with water standpipe 1 on the right, and a track left ahead uphill over a brow which you take.

Water Storage Tank near Kournas Lake

Continue over the brow for 60m to meet another track going down right ahead bearing right and left uphill bearing left which you take, passing a small model stone shrine on the left.

Continue ahead for 60m to meet a fork going down right ahead bearing left and fork ahead left uphill which you take, passing water standpipe 2 on the left.

Continue 130m to a large round concrete water storage tank on the left.

Crete Walks in the Apokoronas

You can look into this tank by climbing the iron steps on the left, but you cannot walk around it as the path is blocked.

Continue along this wide easy track for 1.5km, passing in sequence on the right: water standpipes 3, 4, 5, 5A (opposite an interesting Austrian-style of property on the left), 20 and 21.

Eventually arrive at T-junction, with water standpipe 22 opposite, with a tarmac road going down right and up left over a brow bearing left which you take. Continue for 200m along this tarmac road to reach a track going off left bearing right which you take.

Continue along this level winding track for 500m to a fork ahead left uphill bearing right and fork ahead right downhill bearing right which you take, to soon cross over a little bridge.

Continue uphill ahead to the bottom of Mouri village. Pass the small village church on the left to meet a tarmac road (1) going uphill left over a brow and back down right which you take to return to the parking place on the left that was the start of the walk.

Kournas Lake

After the walk, you could visit Kournas Lake and its tavernas which are close by. To do so, drive up the hill, take the fork ahead right, proceed 500m down to a crossroads which you then cross over. Drive down the hill to one of the many free car parking areas and enjoy the freshwater lake and its tavernas.

WALK 16

NEO CHORIO – MACHERI - NEROCHORI

7.5 km or 9 km – 2.5 hours or 4 hours

The Walk
This circular walk leaves the outskirts of Neo Chorio to make its way through a number of quiet lanes and tracks to the picturesque village of Macheri that nestles below a high cliff. This village has many old and interesting properties lining the main street through the village, and a traditional kafenion in its small square.

There is a small church set high above the village, in the hillside, from where there are some great views. The walk then proceeds through more quiet tracks and lanes to the next village of Nerochori. The walk passes the ruins of a small Turkish fort located on the top of a hill, also having great views around, before returning back down to Neo Chorio.

Take a small towel in case a shallow ford you have to cross has some water flowing after rain.

The Terrain
This walk is along a mixture of tarmac, concrete, gravel and grassy vehicular tracks. There is a 500m section towards the fort that is over some grass surfaces with no clearly discernable track to follow, but the descriptions below will guide you through.

The gradients on the main walk vary throughout from easy to moderate. There is one steep climb for 250m to reach a tarmac road, and there is a 150m steep descent after Nerochori on a narrow winding grassy track.

The Start
If coming from Kalyves, proceed on the road through Armeni and through Neo Chorio where you bear left uphill and follow the sign to Rethymnon. Proceed a further 1km, passing the first right bend after the village of Neo Chorio, to find a lay-by on the right where you can park.

If coming from Agioi Pantes, park in the lay-by on the left immediately after passing the 'entering Neo Chorio' sign on the right.

****

Crete Walks in the Apokoronas

Start walking downhill towards Neo Chorio, bearing left from the lay-by - note the picturesque village of Macheri nestling below the hillside on the left. After a 120m section of straight road bear slightly right – at this bend there are some stone steps on the right going up to a small but interesting cave church.

Continue down the next 220m section of straight road. Reach a traffic observation mirror on the left opposite a narrow lane going back right uphill (1). Continue ahead bearing slightly right to reach a SHELL petrol sign on the right, 20m after which you take the track going back left downhill.

Continue 60m to the bottom of the track to reach a fork ahead left uphill and a fork ahead right downhill which you take. Soon reach a small dip which can become a shallow ford after heavy rain.

Continue uphill from the dip bearing right, passing water standpipe 324 on the right. Soon reach a property on the right immediately before a tarmac road crossing ahead right downhill and back left uphill bearing right, with a track directly ahead bearing left which you take.

Ford in Winter Flow after Heavy Rain

Continue ahead on the track as it ascends through an olive grove for 350m. Reach a junction that has a minor track going ahead bearing left downhill, and a tarmac lane that crosses right downhill and left bearing right which you take. Follow this tarmac lane for 350m, passing two sets of steel gates on opposite sides of the lane.

Crete Walks in the Apokoronas

Reach another junction with a tarmac lane that crosses left and right uphill bearing right, with a track ahead downhill which you take bearing right.

Continue through a dip going across a riverbed, and ascend the other side bearing right. After 110m reach a minor track going directly ahead which you ignore to continue on the main track as it bears right uphill.

Continue 120m up the hill to reach an unmarked water standpipe on the left followed by fork ahead left over a brow and a fork ahead right uphill which you take. Pass a cemetery and chapel on the left. Continue to a T-junction with a track going right downhill and left uphill which you take.

Continue uphill ahead, ignoring the tarmac lane going ahead left downhill bearing right, soon to enter the small square of Macheri village with its modern amphitheatre on the left. This is a good place to stop for a break as you look out over the valley towards the ruined castle on the hill.

Macheri Village

With the amphitheatre on your left, leave the square by the lane going uphill ahead. Reach the second narrow lane off right with a signpost to "ΠΡΟΣ ΑΓ. ΙΩΑΝΝΗ". This is the Church of St. Ioannis that can be seen on the hillside above.

Crete Walks in the Apokoronas

Option: To visit the hillside church above
It does not look possible to reach the church from there but it is, although it is not an easy climb. The views from the church are worth the effort, but care is required to reach it as follows:

Meander up over steps and round narrow bends, passing a couple of old properties and chicken runs, to get above all the properties. Then veer to the right onto the bottom of a rough path, aiming to get between the middle of two old scraggly trees that are in front of you. Continue up this path as it zigzags all the way up to the church ahead of you. After visiting the church and taking in the splendid panoramic views, retrace your steps back down to the lane and turn right.

Continue to follow the lane as it meanders through and out of the village, passing many old and interesting properties along the way. Reach and ignore a tarmac lane going back left downhill, 50m after which there is a track off ahead right uphill.

Option: To visit a small cave church (adding 1.2km to the walk)
This track going off right uphill leads after 600m to a delightful little church set in the mouth of a cave. There are splendid views of a gorge below as you ascend to the church. After visiting the church, retrace your steps back down to the road, turn right and continue below.

Continue to follow the lane as it winds its way to a sharp left-hand hairpin bend, passing a small cave on the right. Eventually reach a junction with another track going ahead left downhill and right uphill bearing left then right - where you have the following option.

Cave Church, outside Macheri

Crete Walks in the Apokoronas

Option: To shorten the walk to 7.5km, omitting Nerochori village
Turn left, then after 40m turn right onto a track which soon bears right. Follow the main course of this track to its end as it ascends up to a bend in a tarmac road that goes ahead left and back right bearing left which you take. Very carefully follow the left side of this busy tarmac road (to face oncoming traffic) for 300m until you reach water standpipe 499 on the left, then take the track going left uphill immediately before it.

Then follow the directions from paragraph **E** on page 99.

To continue the walk to the village of Nerochori, turn right uphill bearing left then right. Continue down to a dip with a minor fork ahead left uphill bearing right and a tarmac lane going ahead right uphill which you take.

Continue 750m to the end of this tarmac lane. Reach a junction with a tarmac road crossing right uphill bearing left into the village of Paidohori and left downhill bearing left which you take, ignoring the minor lane going ahead left over a brow.

Ignore after 40m a minor lane going directly ahead as you turn 45° left. Continue 350m on the main course of this tarmac lane into the small village signed as "Nerochori".

Reach a church directly ahead as the road turns through two left corners, 30m apart, before it exits the village bearing right downhill which you take.

Continue bearing right downhill to reach a church on the left and cemetery on the right. After a further 60m reach a track ahead left downhill which you take.

Follow this narrow track to a sharp right-hand bend which you ignore to take the very minor track going ahead steeply downhill through an olive grove. After 110m you will reach a fork ahead right downhill, but the main track to take goes ahead even steeper downhill bearing left.

Continue down the track a further 110m to reach a concrete bridge over a riverbed, immediately before which is a concrete hut on the left that is beside a short narrow lane leading to a small church. Cross over the bridge and climb the 250m track going ahead uphill.

Crete Walks in the Apokoronas

Reach a tarmac road going left bearing right and right bearing left, with water standpipe 499 across the road and a track bearing left uphill beside it which you take.

E Continue on the main course of this track for 370m to reach an area of beehives on the left, after which the track bears slightly right towards a brow.

Continue ahead for a further 150m, keeping a wire fence on the right. Reach a point where the main track turns sharp left downhill bearing left (there may also be a black water pipe with orange stripes crossing the ground in front of you). Directly in front of you there is what looks like a low brow of stones and soil which you now cross over.

Continue ahead on this rough grass track for 200m, noting on you right side as you bear gently round to the left:
- a short distance of wire fence,
- a short distance of stone wall,
- another short distance of wire fence,

before reaching a stone wall crossing left to right ahead of you and the remains of two old buildings on the right.

Turkish Fort, Neo Chorio

Crete Walks in the Apokoronas

Cross over a low section in the stone wall that is facing you to enter a fenced area. Walk 130m through to its far end, heading towards the castle ruins that are in front on you.

On reaching the far end of the enclosure, pass through a stock fence forming the centre section of a wire fence to enter a small enclosed olive grove.

Continue towards the castle ahead, leaving the olive grove through yet another stock fence, to reach after 15m a track going left downhill bearing left and right uphill bearing right.

Please note that the whole area of the ruins of the Turkish fort is not safe and you leave the track to visit it at your own risk.

To proceed with the walk follow the track in the opposite direction to Macheri village. Reach a sharp left-hand bend in front of black gates which you pass to descend bearing right then left downhill.

Continue to the bottom of the winding hill to reach a junction with a tarmac road going right uphill bearing right and left downhill bearing left which you take, ignoring after 60m a tarmac road going left uphill.

Continue down a further 60m to meet a tarmac road going right downhill bearing left and ahead left uphill bearing right which you take, passing a small pumping station on the right.

Continue passed a large cemetery and church on the right. Reach a fork ahead left and a fork ahead right downhill which you take, then after 30m take the lane back left downhill bearing right.

Continue for 500m on the main course of this lane, ignoring any turnings off to the left or right, as it descends to a dip and ascends ahead and over a brow bearing right.

Continue to the bottom of the hill to a junction with a tarmac road (1) going right downhill bearing right and left uphill which you take.

Reach after 400m the lay-by on the right which was the starting point of the walk.

Crete Walks in the Apokoronas

WALK 17

NIPPOS - Countryside to the South East

5 km or 7 km – 1.5 hours or 2 hours

The Walk
This mostly circular walk meanders down from Nippos along quiet tracks to reach a small church and picnic area in the middle of nowhere (the end point of the short walk).

The walk then continues on other quiet tracks/lanes to pass a small 15th century church before reaching the furthest point at a Roman humpback bridge outside Vryses. The walk then returns on different quiet tracks and lanes.

Take a small towel in case a shallow ford you have to cross has some water flowing after rain.

The Terrain
Various surfaces ranging from gravel tracks to some short stretches of quiet tarmac road. Gradients range from long sections of level to moderate, with some short steep sections going uphill or downhill.

The Start
Take the road from Vryses towards Vafes. After 0.5km take the right turn signposted to "Νιππος 4" (i.e. Nippos 4). Proceed up the hill into Nippos. Park somewhere conveniently near the war memorial on the left, or in the vicinity of the well-respected local 'ΤΑΒΕΡΝΑ ΙΠΠΟΚΟΡΩΝΙΟΝ'.

****

With the war memorial on your right and taverna on your left, proceed 120m downhill. Reach a building on the right, at a curious angle to the road with four louvered windows at the front, and a narrow lane going back right downhill immediately in front of it which you take.

Continue along the main course this narrow winding lane. Pass property No. 128 on the right to proceed downhill through a left-right joggle to emerge onto the end of a tarmac lane. Follow the lane as it goes uphill bearing left passed a church on the right and over a brow.

Crete Walks in the Apokoronas

Continue a short distance further into the next dip. Ignore the main course of the tarmac lane going ahead left uphill and take the minor track going ahead downhill. Reach a tarmac road at the bottom that goes back right over a brow and ahead left downhill which you take.

After 100m take the concrete track going ahead right downhill and continue to the bottom of the dip, which may be a shallow ford after heavy rains, then ascend the other side bearing right, ignoring a track going ahead left uphill very soon after.

Continue on the main course of this winding track for 600m, ignoring a minor fork ahead left as you go over a brow bearing ahead right downhill.

Church in the Middle of Nowhere

Eventually reach a large clearing with a white church ahead, two very large trees, some concrete picnic seats and tables, and three other tracks going: 1) left onto a tarmac road, 2) right bearing right, 3) directly ahead.

Proceed out of the clearing on the above track 3) going directly ahead, soon to pass an un-numbered water standpipe on the right and water standpipe 608A on the left.

Crete Walks in the Apokoronas

Continue on the main course of this track for a further 800m to reach a junction with four other tracks going: 1) back right downhill, 2) ahead right uphill, 3) left downhill, 4) ahead immediately after water standpipe 608 on its right corner.

Option: To shorten to walk to 5km
Take the above track 3) going left downhill to its end where it bears right before joining a tarmac road going ahead right and back left which you take, then follow the directions from point **F** on Page 104.

To continue with the full walk, proceed on the above track 4) going ahead downhill immediately after water standpipe 608 on its right corner.

Continue on the main course of this track to arrive at a two-tier dry stone wall on the right, after which there is an entrance back right through two steel gates to the small and interesting church of "Αγιοι Ασωματοι" (Holy Angels) which is a 'must see' feature of the walk. There are detailed notices in its grounds giving its history.

After visiting the church, return to the lane and turn right. Follow the lane for 600m to a T-junction (2) with a tarmac lane going left downhill and right which you take.

Roman Humpback Bridge, Vryses

Crete Walks in the Apokoronas

After 50m you reach a junction with the Vryses to Vafes main road. Carefully cross over the road and continue along the lane directly ahead for 150m to reach a humpback bridge called "Elliniki Kamara" (i.e. "Greek Arch") from the Roman period (67BC - 395AD).

Retrace your steps back to the Vryses to Vafes main road. Carefully cross over it again and follow the track directly ahead, passing after 50m the left turning uphill (2) signposted to 'Άγιοι Ασωματοι' which you now ignore.

Continue ahead for 700m, passing along the way on the right:

- Water standpipes 402A and then 601,
- After a further 120m the stump of an enormous tree of diameter 1.5m that has been sawn down to its base (one can only imagine how tall it must have been before it was cut down),
- Water standpipe labelled 601 but is painted 601A.

Eventually reach a concrete wall on the left before of a junction of four other tracks going: 1) ahead left immediately bearing left, 2) back right bearing left, 3) ahead right uphill bearing right, and: 4) the tarmac lane continuing generally ahead which you follow.

F Continue ahead on the tarmac lane for 300m, passing water standpipe 611 on the right, to reach a track off back right which you ignore to re-enter the large clearing (1) with the white church on your left and the three other tracks now going: 1) left bearing left, 2) ahead right uphill, and: 3) directly ahead passed the second large tree which you take.

Continue ahead on this track, passing an un-numbered water standpipe on the left, followed 10m after by a track off right uphill bearing left which you take. Pass a large property on the right behind a sliding gate.

Continue ahead for 600m, ignoring a track forking back left downhill in the middle of a small dip, to reach a junction with the Vafes to Nippos road going left and right which you take.

Proceed 170m along the tarmac road to where it turns sharp right, then continue on the minor track directly ahead bearing right, ignoring after 20m another track going off left steeply uphill with water standpipe Γ9 in the near left corner.

Crete Walks in the Apokoronas

Continue for 300m on the main course of this track, passing water standpipes Γ8 and Γ7 on the left, to reach water standpipe Γ6 facing with a minor track going right downhill which you ignore to continue on the main course of the track going ahead left uphill.

Roman Humpback Bridge, Vryses

Continue on the concrete track ahead, climbing up the quite steep gradient for 110m to reach water standpipes Γ5 on the right where the gradient becomes less steep.

Continue ahead to pass water standpipe Γ4 on the left at a right bend which you follow. Reach water standpipes Γ3 and Γ2 on the left.

Continue over the brow, ignoring the right turn, to follow the narrow lane ahead downhill for 200m to the bottom. Then ascend quite steeply for another 200m to reach a junction with the Nippos to Tzitzifes road going left and right uphill which you take.

Pass a small church on the right as you bear right before arriving back at the war memorial and taverna which were at the starting point of the walk.

Crete Walks in the Apokoronas

WALK 18

PERMONIA - FRES

7 km – 2.5 hours

The Walk
This mostly circular walk passes through Permonia then out into the countryside of shallow valleys and wooded areas to follow quiet tracks into Fres main square.

The walk then follows other similar tracks through the countryside back to Permonia.

When in Fres, there is an option to visit two small but very interesting churches at the top of Fres – See Walk 8 on page 63.

The Terrain
Mostly on minor vehicular tracks that are mostly of gravel, with some of the route being along tarmac or concrete lanes. All are easy underfoot. The gradients are level or moderate.

The Start
If heading from Vamos:
> Proceed along the road from Vamos to Agioi Pantes. Cross the bridge over the National Highway to meet a T-junction where you turn right signposted to "Chania 26". After 70m take the turning left, just after the kafenion ΠΑΡΑΔΟΕΙΑΚΟ ΚΑΦΕΝΕΙΟ, that is signposted to "Melidoni 5". Proceed ahead 1.6km to pass the "entering Permonia" sign on the right, then reaching the bottom of the hill where you can park in a clearing on the left, before the road rises again into Permonia.

If heading from the National Highway:
> Turn off for Agioi Pantes. Proceed 50m down to a crossroads which you go across ahead and follow the road signposted to "Melidoni 5". Proceed ahead 1.6km to pass the "entering Permonia" sign on the right, then reaching the bottom of the hill where you can park in a clearing on the left, before the road rises again into Permonia.

****

With the clearing on your left, proceed uphill for 100m towards the village. Follow the main road round to the left, passing the large plane tree in the middle of the road on your right. Continue on the road ahead, go over the first brow, then ignore the turning off ahead right uphill signposted to Fres and Melidoni.

Continue a further 15m and turn down the narrow lane going left downhill between properties. Proceed to the bottom of this track to reach a tarmac road (1) going across left to right downhill with a water standpipe in the near right corner, and a track ahead bearing left downhill which you take.

Continue 300m along the main course of this track, passing an old rectangular stone shepherds hut on the left, to arrive at a small clearing ahead with a fork ahead left which you ignore, and a fork ahead right which you take to bear right after 20m.

Continue ahead on the main course of this winding track for 800m, passing along the way a small bridge carrying a number of water pipes, and a stone/concrete base on the left.

Pass through an almost 180° double-left bend with a track off back right into an olive grove, followed immediately after by an old stone wall on the right.

Eventually reach a T-junction, with water standpipe 486 opposite, and a track going back left downhill and quite steeply ahead right uphill which you take.

Climb the track for 300m to reach at a T-junction at the top of the hill, with water standpipe 487 in the left corner, and a track going left uphill and right uphill bearing left which you take.

Continue for 380m on the main course of the track ahead, passing some large agave plants on the right, then an old well in a small concrete enclosure, to reach a playground area followed by a small square. Proceed to the far end of the small square (2) and leave by the short lane at the far right corner. Continue to the T-junction and turn left.

Pass the large church of Fres on the right to join the main tarmac road through the village. Turn right and follow the main road uphill to the T-junction where you turn left to enter Fres main square.

Crete Walks in the Apokoronas

Main Square in Fres

To visit two small churches at the top of Fres, departing from Fres square, see Walk 8 on Page63.

To resume this walk from Fres main square, retrace your steps back to the small square (2) above as follows: With the arched exit from the main square behind you, leave by lane at the far left corner, then take the first right to follow the main road downhill towards the large church.

Walk round the church to the far side and follow the lane passed the iron gates of the church, now on your left, to take the first lane going down right. Continue a short distance down that lane to re-enter the small square (2).

Walk to the far right end of the fenced playground area and take the track going off right and then almost immediately left downhill.

Continue ahead for 600m as the track winds its way downhill to a T-junction going back right downhill and ahead left downhill which you take.

Crete Walks in the Apokoronas

Continue ahead for 600m, passing a fork back right uphill at water standpipe 480A, and a second track off ahead right uphill, to reach the bottom of the hill at a fork back right bearing left and a fork left ahead which you take.

Then after just 5m ignore another fork right ahead to continue ahead bearing left, immediately passing a large walnut tree on the right corner.

Continue ahead for 550m, passing large agave plants and water standpipes 481 and 482 on the right, to reach a junction of tracks that go ahead left bearing left, ahead bearing right, and right uphill bearing left which you take.

Pass water standpipe 485 on the right. Continue uphill to a T-junction going back right uphill and down left ahead which you take. Continue ahead to pass through a dip and ignore a track 20m after going left downhill bearing right.

Reach a T-junction with a tarmac lane going ahead right and left bearing left which you take.

Continue round a number of bends. Pass an unmarked water standpipe on the left as you continue ahead bearing right. Go over a brow to arrive at a junction with a track going back left downhill, a minor track opposite going down a dip, and the main course of the tarmac lane you are on going ahead right which you take. Pass a water standpipe on the right and an old stone wall on the left as you go over a brow.

Continue round some more bends to again reach the junction (1), with a track going left downhill bearing left, the tarmac road going ahead downhill bearing right, and a minor track going right which you take.

Retrace your steps back up the lane ahead to the T-junction with a tarmac road where you turn right. Proceed along the road for 180m, passing over the brow, to eventually reach the sharp right corner with the large plane tree in the middle of the road where you now turn right.

Follow the road for 100m back down to the parking area on the right which was the starting point of the walk.

Crete Walks in the Apokoronas

WALK 19

PLAKA - Coastline

4 km or 6 km – 1.5 or 2 hours

The Walk
This 'figure of eight' walk leaves Plaka square to go through quiet olive groves as it meanders down to a sections of rocky coastline, then to skirt round a ravine to arrive at a quiet promontory with great views. The return back up to Plaka is through more olive groves.

The Terrain
Mostly on gravel tracks in the countryside, and with tarmac lanes in the Plaka area. Gradients are moderate with some short steeper sections.

The Start
Plaka square.

****

Start at the bottom of Plaka square, with the "Η ΠΛΑΚΑ" supermarket on your right, and the bus shelter and telephone booth behind you. Proceed on the road down hill bearing left towards Almyrida. After 60m take the right turn at the signpost to the Bicorna Garden Cafe.

Rocky Coastline on Walk

Crete Walks in the Apokoronas

Continue 40m to a T-junction and turn right over a brow. Continue 160m through a dip to reach a right turn uphill which you ignore and a lane ahead downhill which you take.

Continue 400m on the main course of this lane, passing water standpipe 263 on the left, to reach a junction with a track going back left and ahead right bearing left which you take, immediately passing a small shrine to ΑΓΙΑ ΑΝΝΑ (St Anna) on your left.

Continue 420m along the main course of this track, passing water standpipes 265 and 266 on you right, to reach a fork ahead right bearing left and a track ahead downhill which you take.

Continue downhill on the gravel track bearing right for 850m to follow the rocky coastline. Reach a back left downhill track to a large property below.

> *Down this short track and round to the left are some small caves and in summer some salt pools. The path down to these is not easy.*

Continue 500m along the main track bearing right away from the coastline to reach a junction with another track going back right and ahead left which you take. Continue ahead 250m to reach a junction of tracks (1), with water standpipe 271 in the far right corner.

Option – To shorten walk to 4km
Continue ahead across this junction of tracks and continue directions from paragraph **G** on page 112.

To continue the full walk, turn left bearing right and follow the main course of this track for 450m, passing water standpipe 272A on the right. Reach a track going right bearing right, with water standpipe 274 in the right corner, and left downhill bearing right which you take.

Continue on the main course of this track for 330m as you descend, passing water standpipe 276 on the right, to reach a track off right uphill (2) over a brow which you ignore to continue ahead downhill.

Continue for 350m along this track as it follows the rocky coastline. Reach the end of the track at a fenced off clearing with amazing views and some ruined stone buildings. This area is a great place to stop for a picnic.

Crete Walks in the Apokoronas

Retrace your steps back up to the junction with track (2) above, now appearing left uphill over a brow bearing right which you take – if you reach water standpipe 276 on the left you have gone too far!

Continue 350m along the main course of this track to reach a T-junction going left downhill and right uphill which you take.

View on Walk

Continue 500m along the main course of this winding and undulating track to reach a track going back right bearing left over a brow and ahead left downhill which you take. Reach a junction of two tracks (1), with water standpipe 271 in the far left corner, where you turn left.

G Continue 200m to reach two staggered junctions, the first off left, the second after 3m going back right uphill which you take. Continue uphill into the outskirts of Plaka. Reach a T-junction where you bear left, then immediately bear right as you ignore a cul-de-sac on the left.

Proceed for 100m through this winding lane to reach another T-junction going ahead left, and right downhill in front of a large eucalyptus tree which you take. Proceed along the lane ahead, passing a large church on your right, to re-enter Plaka square which was the start of the walk.

WALK 20

RAMNI – Foothills of the White Mountains & Two Churches

3.5 km and/or 8 km – 1.5 hours and/or 2.5 hours

The Walk
This walk consists of two single-ended parts, A and B, which can be walked separately or combined from the same starting point.

Part A - This walk makes its way along quite tracks, alongside a riverbed through a gorge, then through a disused football pitch in the middle of nowhere, then along a lane that climbs up to the small church of Ayios Nikolaos outside Ramni that has some nice views around.

Part B - This walk makes its way up to the small village of Tsakistra in the foothills of the White Mountains, to reach a modern Byzantine-style church with great views of the countryside around (gorges, valleys, mountains, sea, etc.) as does the route all the way up to it.

The Terrain

Part A - Along easy gravel or grassy vehicular tracks for the first half that are more or less level. The second half is along a concrete vehicular track that ascends steeply to the church.

Part B - Along two quiet tarmac roads all the way to the top, with gradients that are gentle all the way.

The Start for Both Walks A and B
Drive to the hillside village of Ramni. Enter its small main square with the large white church and its four-sided clock tower. With the church on your left, proceed out of the square following the sign turning left to "Kares, Kyriakoselia, etc".

After 200m, turn down the lane going back right that is signposted to "Chiliomoudou, Kyriakoselia, etc". After 700m, reach the bottom of the hill at a concrete bridge over a riverbed. Park somewhere conveniently near the bridge on one of the small areas at the road side.

****

Crete Walks in the Apokoronas

Part A

Start the walk from the T-junction immediately across the concrete bridge. With the riverbed on your left, proceed ahead 20m and take the track ahead left downhill that crosses the riverbed.

Continue ahead for 500m along the vehicular track with the riverbed on your right, ignoring a fork ahead right into a dip that crosses the riverbed, to reach a point where you cross the riverbed.

Bear left uphill and pass through some rusty gates onto a disused gravel football pitch. Proceed across the pitch and leave through another set of gates to the left of the building at the far end.

Follow the main course of the vehicular track for 160m after leaving the pitch, immediately passing over a small bridge across the riverbed, to reach a junction in front of a water standpipe with a track going back left uphill bearing right and ahead right bearing right which you take.

Ignore a track off ahead left uphill after just 20m.

Track leading to the Church of Ayios Nikolaos, near Ramni

Continue on the main course of this concrete track for 1km as it winds its way increasingly steeply uphill to reach the small church at the top which has some nice views around.

Crete Walks in the Apokoronas

When ready to return, retrace your steps along the concrete track back down to the bottom. At the junction with the water standpipe on the right, turn left ahead bearing left. Pass back through the football pitch, leaving through the goalpost at the far end.

Retrace your steps back along the vehicular track with the riverbed on your left, to arrive back at the concrete bridge at the bottom which was the starting point of the walk.

Part B

Start the walk from the T-junction immediately across the concrete bridge. With the riverbed on your left, proceed ahead, ignoring after 20m the track ahead left downhill that crosses the riverbed.

Continue to follow the main course of the winding tarmac lane uphill for 2.5km, enjoying some great views of the changing countryside all around. Eventually reach a brow bearing left between two rocks to see a white Byzantine-style church high above you on the hill ahead.

View towards Drapanos from the Church in Tsakistra

Continue ahead for 750m, through a short dip, to ascend to a second brow at a T-junction (1) with a road going left downhill bearing left signposted to "Madaro 1" and right uphill bearing left signposted to "Campoi 3" which you take.

Crete Walks in the Apokoronas

Proceed along the winding road for 400m. Reach a fork back right uphill which you take to arrive at the white Byzantine-style church which is the endpoint of this walk.

View towards Ramni from the Church in Tsakistra

This endpoint is a good place to stop for a break and enjoy some great views around. You are now in the village of Tsakistra.

When ready to return, retrace your steps back to the T-junction (1) with the road to Madaro, then turn left downhill.

> *The dead-end road to the village of Madaro leads to a mountain track going a further 8km up to the Volikas Shelter at an altitude of 1350m on the western slopes of the White Mountains. The is Walk 43 in the second book "More Crete Walks in the Apokoronas"*

Continue along the road as it winds its way downhill to arrive back at the concrete bridge at the bottom which was the starting point of the walk.

WALK 21

STYLOS - DIKTAMOS GORGE

6 km or 9,5 km – 1.5 hours or 3 hours

The Walk
This circular walk starts from Stylos, a village very fortunate in having a number of freshwater springs and small streams flowing nearby. After a stroll through the village, passing some of the flowing streams and tavernas along the main street, the walk follows quiet country tracks through orange and olive groves before crossing a small river (see Walk 4 on page 45 which meets this river 900m further downstream).

The walk then follows a smaller stream through more orange groves to reach a section of river bank, although this particular river is likely to be dry. A short section of tarmac road picks up a quiet lane leading to the picturesque ruin of an old Byzantine church.

After returning to the tarmac road, with an option there to shorten the walk to 6km, the full walk continues along another section of the river bank. After this there is second option to walk into the bottom of the Diktamos Gorge. The walk then continues along more quiet tracks and lanes over two hills before dropping back down into Stylos.

Take a small towel in case a shallow ford you have to cross has some water flowing after rain.

The Terrain
This walk is along a variety of surfaces that are easy to walk over, but the optional extended walk into the Diktamos Gorge is over rocks and boulders in some parts. The shortened walk of 6km crosses over a low hill at 1km after which it is more or less flat to the end.

The full walk continues along level ground until it passes the mouth of Diktamos Gorge. After that there is a long climb and descent, followed by a second long climb and moderate descent back down to Stylos.

The Start
Outside the large water bottling plant at the northern edge of Stylos.

****

Crete Walks in the Apokoronas

Before starting the walk at the roadside outside the large water bottling plant of Stylos, look at the old church directly opposite called "Church of Ayios Ioannis Theologos". Sadly it is now derelict and locked because it is too dangerous to enter, but there may be a window facing away from the village that is still open through which you can see some areas of old frescos that once adorned the interior. Also, outside in the far left corner near the church is a remarkable fossil of a creature mounted on a stone base (its exact origin is unknown to this day).

Start the walk with the bottling plant on the left. Proceed along the main road through the village bearing left. Pass three very large plane trees on the left, with one of many streams flowing between the 1st and 2nd tree.

Continue bearing right then left to reach a wooden bus shelter on the left, after which you turn left and go down some stone steps into a small wooded area. Proceed generally ahead to reach circular railings inside which is one of the famous Stylos water springs.

Water Spring, Stylos

Behind you is an old football field with rusty goalposts. Walk across this pitch to a small stream. Turn right along the stream to reach a short lane of old properties going left ahead which you follow for 50m.

Turn right at the end of the lane to rejoin the main road where you turn left uphill bearing left over a bridge.

Continue along the road for 190m, bearing right uphill to reach a tarmac lane off ahead left downhill which you take. Continue ahead for 450m, passing a few old properties before entering the countryside, to reach water standpipe 320 on the left. Ignore the fork ahead right uphill to take the track ahead slightly left uphill bearing right.

Continue ahead 150m over a brow, ignoring a track off left bearing left with water standpipe 318B in the far left corner, to continue ahead downhill bearing left.

Continue 190m to a junction with a track ahead bearing right, a tarmac lane going right uphill bearing right, water standpipe 318 in the far left corner, and a tarmac lane going left downhill which you take.

After 210m reach a fork ahead right bearing right, water standpipe 318A facing, and a fork ahead left bearing right which you take. Continue for 210m to ignore a minor fork ahead right, in front of water standpipe 317 on the right, as you bear left.

Streams, Stylos

Crete Walks in the Apokoronas

Pass water standpipe 316 on the left. Continue through a few more bends to cross a concrete bridge over a flowing river, with water standpipe 315 immediately after on the left.

Turn right after the bridge and follow the track ahead for 380m, keeping a smaller stream on your left. Pass water standpipe 314 on the right as you bear right then sharp left over a small bridge to arrive at a junction with a track going left bearing right and right bearing right which you take, immediately passing a breeze block hut on the left.

Continue 550m along the main course of this track, passing water standpipes 312 (painted) and 311 on the left, to reach a shallow ford crossing a riverbed.

Cross over the ford to a junction of tracks going ahead right uphill over a brow bearing left, ahead bearing left, and back left bearing right which you take to follow a track along the riverbank.

Continue 750m on this track following the riverbank to reach a junction, with water standpipe 2XX in the left corner, a track ahead left going across the riverbed, and a bend in the Kalyves to Stylos road that goes back right bearing right and ahead left which you take.

Continue carefully along this tarmac road for 200m to reach a junction (1) with a track ahead left going across the riverbed, the road you are on continuing ahead bearing right, and a lane back right with a signpost for the "Church of Panayia" which you take.

Continue 410m along this lane, passing the White Hill Dogs Home on the left and water standpipe 505 on the right, to reach a track right with another sign to the "Church of Panayia" which you take, arriving at the shell of the Byzantine church after 140m.

> *The church possibly dates back to the 11th century and currently undergoing a prolonged restoration period.*

Retrace your steps back to the above junction (1) with the Kalyves to Stylos road where you now turn right. Continue carefully along this winding tarmac road for 180m to reach another junction, with roads going ahead uphill signed to the "Gorge", back right signed to "Chania", and ahead left signed to "Stylos" which you take, passing water standpipe 5X5 on the left.

Crete Walks in the Apokoronas

Ruin of a Byzantine Church, Stylos

Continue carefully along this tarmac road for 220m bearing left to reach a bridge over the riverbed.

Option: To return to the starting point, reducing the walk to 6km
Continue ahead over the bridge. Follow the tarmac road 800m further to arrive back at the water bottling plant on the left which was the starting point of the walk.

To continue on the full walk, take the narrow track going right downhill immediately in front of the bridge.

Proceed only a short distance to take a fork ahead left going down onto the riverbed. Continue 30m along the riverbed and cross over it to pick up a track going ahead along the left bank which you then follow.

Continue 800m along the track following the left riverbank towards the mouth of Diktamos Gorge, passing along the way water standpipes 519, 517 and 521 on the left, and a property also on the left, to reach a sharp bend in the track (2) going ahead left uphill.

Crete Walks in the Apokoronas

Mouth of Diktamos Gorge

Option: To enter Diktamos Gorge for up to 1km (additional)
The Diktamos Gorge is 5km long. It is not an easy gorge to walk for its full length, however the first 1km is relatively easy and accessible. After that the going gets tortuous and potentially dangerously and it is not recommended for the casual tourist. To venture into the first part of the gorge, continue ahead on the minor track leading down onto the riverbed and carefully make your way along it. The first obvious obstruction you reach is four very large rocks across your path. Pass to the left side of these following the red arrow. The next obvious obstruction you reach is a dip with one extremely large rock apparently blocking your path. The author does not advise you to progress any further than this point as to continue is potentially hazardous. Retrace your steps back to the bend in the main track (2) above and continue the walk from there. The author recommends the much more tourist-friendly and picturesque 7km Imbros Gorge on the south of Crete, near Hora Sfakion. It also has a great historical significance for the part it played in the Battle of Crete during the Second World War.

The Imbros Gorge is Walk 37 in the second book "More Crete Walks in the Apokoronas"

Crete Walks in the Apokoronas

To continue the walk, proceed uphill for 230m along the main track leaving the riverbed behind you. Pass through a left then a right bend to reach a small church on the right.

This church was under construction in December 2009.

Continue uphill to reach a track going ahead right uphill and a track going left uphill over a brow which you take. Continue along the main course of this track for 650m, passing along your way a deep dip, a white shrine on the right as you ascend, a stone threshing circle (aloni) at a right-hand corner, to eventually reach a brow as you pass through the centre of a small village bearing left.

Descend 70m to an open area, with a lane forking ahead left bearing left which you ignore. Continue ahead downhill bearing right then left.

Continue 410m downhill on the main course of this road to reach a junction with a tarmac lane going ahead right uphill, the main road going ahead downhill bearing left, and a lane going back left downhill towards properties which you take.

Follow the main course of this lane downhill for 100m. Reach a narrow gap between two properties, the one on the right having a number of steel gates, after which you turn left over a brow.

Continue 170m along this lane, passing a number of old properties and going through three close bends (right-left-right) to arrive at the bottom of the hill where the main course of the lane bears right.

Continue downhill along this now tarmac road for 120m as it bears round to the left, ignoring the turnings off to the right until you pass a property on the right with an arched entrance into a courtyard behind. Here you ignore the main course of the road going left downhill into a 30km/h area to immediately turn right downhill into a lane.

Continue 110m down the main course of this lane, passing a large church on the left to reach the main road through Stylos.

Turn left and follow the main road for 160m, passing a number of tavernas along the way, to reach the water bottling factory on the right which was the starting point of the walk.

Crete Walks in the Apokoronas

WALK 22

VAFES – VOTHONAS PLATEAU

12 km – 3.5 hours

The Walk
This circular walk leaves the village of Vafes to climb steadily up to the foothills of the White Mountains to reach the fertile Vothonas Plateau. The walk then descends back to the outskirts of Tzitzifes and down a valley back to Vafes. This long walk has some nice views along its route.

For an easier and shorter single-ended walk (7km, 2hours) up to the Vothonas Plateau, see the abbreviated Walk 22A on page 128.

The Terrain
The first part of the walk, after an initial steep gradient through the hairpin bends going out of Vafes, is a steady moderate climb up to the plateau. The first 2.5km are on a tarmac road.

The next 2.5km are on a gravel track that continues the steady climb up to the Vothonas Plateau that is at 580m above sea level.

After passing through the level plateau, the walk continues for 6km on tracks with various surfaces and descending gradients to pass the outskirts of Tzitzifes, before arriving back in Vafes.

Although most of the tracks are easy underfoot, there are a few sections where these tracks are stony or have loose gravel on the surface.

The Start
From Vryses, take the road out to Vafes. As lack of parking space in Vafes village is a problem, continue to follow the main road through Vafes, passing the war memorial on the left.

Proceed to climb out of Vafes village. After the first sharp left hairpin bend (1), park in the clearing on the left immediately after it, or somewhere convenient near by.

****

Crete Walks in the Apokoronas

To start the walk, turn left from the clearing. Proceed to follow this one tarmac road uphill for 2.5km as it twists and turns its way uphill, passing a deep gorge and small hilltop chapel on the left, and then a number of dwellings that form the hamlet of Arevitis up on the right.

Eventually, about 100m after passing the hamlet of Arevitis, reach a sharp bend going back right uphill towards that hamlet, with a gravel track going ahead uphill bearing left which you take.

Vafes Village

Follow the main course of the gravel track for 2.5km as it twists and turns uphill, passing two livestock sheds on the right before it descends a second brow onto the large flat fertile Vothonas plateau. Proceed to the other end of the plateau, noting the low square stone-covered water well on the left after 240m. Reach a junction with a fork ahead left uphill bearing left and a fork ahead right uphill sweeping back right.

Option – For even better views and maybe visit a cave church
Take the fork ahead left uphill. Ascend as far as you comfortably want to go along this 3.5km dead-end track. You will be rewarded with some amazing views of the surrounding landscape far off into the distance.

A sign at the start of this track points to an interesting cave church dedicated to Saints Peter & Paul that is located at the end of the track, hidden in amongst a small clump of trees. It leaves you wondering why such delightful churches are built in the most unusual and remote places. To reach the church will add another 7km onto the walk.

Crete Walks in the Apokoronas

To continue the walk from the end of the plateau, take the fork ahead right uphill that sweeps back right. Follow this track for 600m as it winds its way round to the left to reach a right bend in the track which you take, ignoring the minor track going ahead uphill bearing right.

Vothonas Plateau

After 240m reach a T-junction with a track going left uphill and down right which you take. Continue on the main course of this long and winding track for 4km, noting the following as you descend:

- The 14 (approximately!) hairpin bends that you pass through,
- Nippos village coming into view directly ahead, then:
- Tzitzifes village coming into view below on the right, then:
- Fres village coming into view in the distance ahead, then:
- A livestock building on the right at the last left hairpin bend.

Eventually reach a junction at the bottom with a tarmac lane going level ahead and almost completely backwards bearing right uphill which you take.

Follow the main course of this track for 500m to reach a fork ahead left downhill bearing right and a fork ahead right downhill bearing right which you take.

Crete Walks in the Apokoronas

Continue 400m along the main course of this winding and undulating track to reach, after a gentle right bend, a sharp back left bend downhill which you must follow - you cannot proceed ahead!

Continue descending this track for 650m to the bottom of the valley, passing some old stone water troughs on your right along the way.

Stone Water Troughs

Continue 350m ahead steeply uphill, ignoring the concrete fork back left downhill going into a small dip. Pass through a right then a left hairpin bend, to reach two metal gates and animal pens on the left, and a junction going ahead left downhill bearing right which you ignore to continue round bearing right.

After 200m reach a sharp back right uphill concrete lane which you take. After only 5m turn sharp left and climb steeply over a brow.

Descend to the bottom of the lane, as it narrows between some old properties, to meet a tarmac lane going ahead left uphill and back right downhill which you take.

After 50m join a tarmac road on a hairpin bend (1) which goes ahead left downhill bearing left and ahead right uphill bearing left which you take to arrive back at the clearing which was the starting point of the walk.

Crete Walks in the Apokoronas

WALK 22A

VOTHONAS PLATEAU (SHORT WALK)

7 km – 2 hours

The Walk

This walk is an abbreviated version of Walk 22 on page 124.

This single-ended walk winds its way steadily along a gravel track up to the foothills of the White Mountains to reach the fertile Vothonas Plateau. The walk then descends back along the same track to the starting point.

The Terrain
The gravel track going up to the plateau has a moderate gradient with some loose gravel in places. The track across the plateau is flat and easy underfoot.

The Start
From Vryses, take the road to Vafes. Proceed through Vafes village and climb through a series of sharp hairpin bends. Proceed on the tarmac road a further 2.5km to reach a sharp right-hand bend going back 100m uphill towards the hamlet of Arevitis, with a gravel track going directly ahead uphill bearing left. Stop near this junction and park.

****

To start the walk, follow the main course of the gravel track going ahead uphill bearing left as it twists and turns uphill for 2.5km. Pass two livestock sheds on the right, before descending a second brow onto the large flat fertile Vothonas plateau.

Proceed 700m along the track across the plateau, noting the low square stone-covered water well on the left after 240m. Reach a junction with a fork ahead left uphill bearing left and a fork ahead right uphill sweeping back right. This junction of tracks is the end point of the walk.

Retrace your steps back to the starting point.

WALK 23

VAMOS – Countryside to the South West

8 km – 2.5 hours

The Walk
This mostly circular walk goes into the countryside to the SW of Vamos. It reaches a small church, set in the ruins of a small monastic settlement that has a number of old frescos still clearly visible on the inside walls.

The walk then goes back to another small church, with good views of the valley below and towards the White Mountains, before meandering through quiet country tracks and through the small village of Metoxi Ghetemi. The walk passes three more small churches with a fourth optional, before arriving back at the starting point.

Take a small towel in case a shallow ford you have to cross has some water flowing after rain.

The Terrain
This walk is mostly over easy tracks of gravel, loose in some places. There is a 300m section of concrete and two sections of tarmac. Gradients are level or moderate all around this walk, apart from the 300m section of concrete in the middle of the walk which is quite steep.

The Start
Outside the main Vamos cemetery.

To get there:

- Leave Vamos main square and proceed downhill towards Kalyves,
- Take the second left turn signed to "Agioi Pantes 5, Kaina 4",
- Proceed through the first left bend and BEFORE it turns right, take the lane off left uphill,
- Follow this lane 100m to the top and turn right, then follow it out of Vamos village,
- Continue to follow this one lane uphill to the church and cemetery on the right, and park there.

****

Crete Walks in the Apokoronas

Start with Vamos village behind you and the cemetery on your right. Proceed up the track ahead for 850m, passing water standpipe 400 on the left and a track back right immediately after it.

Go over the brow, soon to reach a junction with a minor track going off directly ahead downhill which you ignore to follow the main track as it bends ahead left downhill.

Proceed towards the white church visible on the hill ahead. On nearing the church (1), ignore a track off back right downhill and 20m further on a track off ahead right downhill. Continue ahead, passing water standpipe 120A on the left.

Continue 220m on the main track as it gently curves to the left. Reach a track off back right downhill with a sign on the near corner pointing to the "Church of the Koimesis" which you follow.

After 200m you arrive at that church. It is set among the picturesque ruins of a previous monastic settlement and has a number of well-preserved religious frescos inside.

Church of Koimesis, Vamos

Crete Walks in the Apokoronas

Leave the church grounds and retrace your steps back along the track to the junction with the main track. Turn left and proceed back to the first church you passed (1) near water standpipe 120A now on the right.

Stop here to climb the short rough track immediately before water standpipe 120A that goes up to the church above. Although the church is rather Spartan inside, there are some great views from it.

To continue the walk, pass water standpipe 120A on the right, and after 20m take the first track going back left downhill. After 160m reach a left bend. Take the track going off back right downhill that is 10m before water standpipe 117 on the left.

Continue on this track for 620m, ignoring a track off back right uphill as the main track bends round to the left over a brow, and passing water standpipe 120 on the left, to reach a junction with another track going up right and down left which you take, passing water standpipe 121 in the left corner.

Continue for 700m on the main course of this track, passing water standpipes 122, 122A and 122B on the left, to reach a triangular meeting of tracks with an old olive tree in the middle. Take the track sweeping round to the right slightly uphill.

Pass a large flat stone outcrop down in the gulley on the left, as the track drops ahead to a dip which may be a shallow ford after heavy rains.

Cross over the dip and climb the concrete track going 300m uphill. Reach a tarmac road going left downhill, with water standpipe 122Δ on the left corner, and right uphill which you take.

Proceed to follow the tarmac road for 600m as it winds its way up into and through the small village of Metoxi Ghetemi, emerging onto a gravel track to reach a stone circle (aloni) on the left as you go through a left bend.

There is a good location for a picnic over on the left bank.

Continue on the main course of this winding track for 1km, passing a couple of properties on the left, to reach a fork back right downhill and fork left bearing left uphill which you take.

Crete Walks in the Apokoronas

Continue on the main course of this track for 500m to reach a junction with a tarmac road going down left and up right which you take.

Continue along the tarmac road for 550m, passing water standpipe 427 on the right, a small church and water standpipe 425 on the left, to reach a staggered junction of tracks, with water standpipe 423 in the far right corner. Here you take the first track off bearing right.

Continue along this track for 310m to reach an area with a number of stone walls where you take the track off ahead right uphill bearing left. You immediately pass a new church (2006) on the right which is well worth a look inside if it is open.

Continue along this track for about 230m to reaches a low brow, near which you can take the following option.

Optional Diversion to Church of the Black Madonna
Just before the track starts to descend, look out for two large rocks on the left bank, then look out for painted red & blue spots at one point on the stone outcrop on the right side, opposite the second rock. Climb the rocky track going up left to right just in front of the painted spots.

Follow the red/blue painted spots which you now use as markers to guide you along the length of this track as it winds its way for 200m uphill (in the absence of any visible red/blue spots continue generally ahead on the visible path until you meet them again a short distance further on).

After about five minute climbing you reach a rusty steel gate leading to the Church of the Black Madonna. Just before the gate on the right is a small cave shrine. After visiting the church, retrace your steps back to the main track below, enjoying some good views of Vamos on the way down.

Continue over the brow to reach after 450m the end of the track at a junction with another track going up right bearing left and back left downhill, with water standpipe 400 in the left corner.

Turn left and after 130m return to Vamos cemetery which was the starting point of the walk.

WALK 24

VAMOS – Old Village and Countryside to the North West

4 km or 5.5 km – 1.5 hour or 2 hours

The Walk
This circular walk goes through some of the old lanes of Vamos, passing many old properties, before following tracks into the countryside to the NW of the village.

There is an optional single-ended track that climbs 750m further to a higher level that gives some good views of the surrounding countryside as it descends back down.

The route back into Vamos village passes through more of its old lanes.

Vamos is the capital and physical centre of the Apokoronas region. There is a tourist office from where you can get more useful information about the whole area.

The Terrain
The first and last parts of the walk are on tarmac lanes having level or gentle gradients. The middle portion of the walk is over gravel tracks with gradients that vary from level to moderate.

The Start
Vamos main square.

****

Start in Vamos square with the small kiosk on your right. Proceed downhill towards the crossroads and follow the lane directly opposite uphill. Pass Vamos Post Office (ELTA) on the right, then take the first lane going right downhill immediately before the bakery.

Continue down this lane, through a small right-left joggle, to reach a junction of lanes (1) that go right downhill, ahead downhill bearing right, and left downhill which you take.

Then turn into the first lane going right downhill after passing two properties.

Crete Walks in the Apokoronas

Walk just 5m down this lane and turn left into the open entrance signposted "Art Shop (Fabrica)". This building, dated 1840, was used as an olive mill until 1946 and is currently being used for giving cookery lessons. After leaving the entrance, turn right and return up to the front lane, then turn right.

Old Olive Press, Vamos

Proceed to a T-junction with one of the old cobbled roads of Vamos going steeply uphill left and downhill right which you take,

These old cobbled roads were built during the period of Turkish occupation (1669-1898) using the men folk of Vamos as labourers.

Reach another T-junction at the bottom of the hill, going right and left downhill which you take. Follow this short section of cobbled road for 10m, then turn right downhill to meet a T-junction with a tarmac lane going right and left bearing left which you take.

On the left pass the Church of St. George followed by an old primary school that is now used as an exhibition centre.

Continue 200m along this winding tarmac lane, as it bears right then left out of the village, to reach a lane going ahead right downhill which you take, passing water standpipe 405 on the left.

Crete Walks in the Apokoronas

Old Cobbled Road, Vamos

Continue 500m along this winding tarmac lane, ignoring any turnings to the left and the right as it winds its way passed a number of older properties and agricultural plots, to reach a T-junction going left bearing right and ahead right bearing right which you take.

Continue for 140m, passing the Church of the Holy Spirit on the right, to reach a junction with the main Vamos to Kaina road that has a small shrine in the near right corner and a bus shelter in the far left corner.

Carefully cross over the main road and proceed down the lane opposite, to the right of the bus shelter.

Continue along the main course of this winding lane for 1km to its end, passing a number of properties before it becomes a track going out into the countryside, and passing water standpipes 408, 409 and 410 on the right.

Eventually you ascend to a junction (2) with two other tracks, one going ahead left uphill bearing left and the other going back right uphill immediately bearing right.

Crete Walks in the Apokoronas

Option: To shorten the walk to 4km
To make a circular route back to Vamos and omit the best views on this walk, turn back right uphill and immediately bear right, then proceed to paragraph **H** on this page.

To continue with the full walk, take the track going ahead left uphill bearing left – although this is a dead-end track of 750m, and you will have to return back to this junction, you will have some great views of the surrounding countryside on the way back down.

Continue on the main course of this winding track as it ascends, ignoring a turning off ahead right that is opposite a property on the left, and ignoring further along a turning off left uphill over a brow going towards a tall communications mast.

Continue ahead uphill to reach a brow, after which the track passes an olive grove on the right to then disappear 40m further along to make that the endpoint of the walk.

Retrace your steps back down the track, enjoying some great views of the surrounding countryside before you reach the above junction (2) where you then take the track off left immediately bearing right.

H Continue 700m along the main course of this winding track, passing water standpipes 411, 412 and 413 on the left, to reach a turning off left bearing left in front of a low stone wall which you ignore.

Continue on the main track a further 60m, bearing right then left, to ignore another track going off right bearing right towards a large oak tree.

Continue 120m to water standpipe 418 on the left, ignoring the fork ahead left uphill alongside to take the fork ahead right bearing right.

Continue 300m on the main course of this winding lane to reach a junction with the main Vamos to Kaina road with water standpipe 420 in the right corner.

Turn right and carefully follow the main road for 110m, bearing left to a tarmac lane off left uphill which you take. Continue to the top of the hill and turn left.

Crete Walks in the Apokoronas

Follow the narrow tarmac lane for 90m, bearing right and left, to reach a turning off right uphill which you take.

Half way up the hill pass a small church dated 1876. At the top of the hill, turn right then left uphill to again reach the junction of lanes (1) where you now turn right.

After 70m, reach a T-junction where you turn left uphill onto the old stepped cobbled road. After 110m reach the top of the hill with a lane ahead left and a lane ahead right uphill which you take.

Proceed 70m along the lane and take the first left turn. Proceed ahead over the brow, passing the bakery and post office on the left, to reach Vamos square which was the starting point of the walk.

Vamos square is an ideal place to stop for refreshments after the walk.

Vamos Square on a Summer Evening

Crete Walks in the Apokoronas

WALK 25

XIROSTERNI - KEFALAS

6 km – 2 hours

The Walk
This circular walk starts on the outskirts of Xirosterni. The walk follows tracks that meander out into the quiet countryside, through pleasant wooded areas, before ascending up to Kefalas square. The walk then descends along a picturesque track, offering superb views towards the White Mountains and Souda Bay, before going through Xirosterni back to the starting point.

The Terrain
Mostly on tarmac and gravel tracks or lanes, with some tarmac roads. Gradients are mostly level or moderate. There is one short section of old donkey track going down to Xirosterni that passes over small and large stones for up to 100m, but this is negotiable with care. There is one steep climb for 300m on a tarmac road leading up to Kefalas village. One section of the walk negotiates its way carefully through a 200m section of dense woodland.

The Start
From Vamos, drive through Xirosterni towards Kefalas. Shortly after passing the 'exiting Xirosterni' sign on the left, proceed a further 100m and stop outside the church on the right. You can park in the open area in front of the church or down the lane opposite.

****

Start the walk with the small church behind you. Turn left and follow the main road westwards back towards Vamos. Pass the back right downhill turning signposted to "Almyrida 7, Gavalohori 3" and continue ahead towards Vamos for a further 30m only.

Take the tarmac road off left uphill. Continue for 70m and where the road bears round to the right, take the track off ahead left uphill.

Continue 600m along this gravel track as it meanders through the countryside to reach a fork ahead right downhill bearing left and a fork ahead left downhill bearing right which you take.

Crete Walks in the Apokoronas

Continue on this track for 250m, passing through a forest of oak trees, soon to enter a narrow clearing with an old grey stone wall on the left. Here you aim for a half-gap in a tumbling stone wall on the right side which you then pass over to enter a second wider clearing (see Photograph 1).

Photograph 1 - Looking over wall into Second Wider Clearing

Proceed 50m ahead through this wider clearing, aiming towards the far right corner where you turn slightly left (about 5°).

Proceed ahead for another 50m, aiming for the tallest cypress tree ahead with the largest trunk (actually it's one thick main trunk with another thin trunk climbing up close against it).

Pass to the right of this tree to enter a small, old stone-walled enclosure now encircling a number of young cypress trees. Thread your way ahead for 20m to the far corner of this area to reach two very low tumbled-down stone walls crossing in front of you (see Photograph 2).

Cross over the first of these low walls then turn left. Follow the right-hand stone wall for 10m then cross over it at a low point to enter another area of young cypress trees.

Crete Walks in the Apokoronas

Photograph 2 - Two Low Stone Walls in Wood to Cross Over

Thread your way through this wood of young cypress trees, going away from the walls and bearing about 45° left ahead, to meet another low stone wall that is converging with you on your left side.

Turn right ahead and proceed for 60m, keeping this low wall on your left side, until you emerge onto a gravel track going right and left which you take.

Continue 500m on the main course of this track, ignoring a turning off back right in front of a well-built stone wall. Reach a well-defined crossing of two tracks (1) where you can take the following option.

Option – A Picnic Stop
If you want to deviate slightly, for a picnic at a quiet shady spot with some tables and seats, turn right downhill at this junction of tracks. Continue for 250m through a few bends to reach that shady picnic area on the right under a few large trees. To resume the walk retrace our steps back up to the crossing (1) above, turn right and continue below.

Crete Walks in the Apokoronas

Continue ahead for 300m in the same direction as before, eventually to start climbing steeply uphill as you pass a small two-storey concrete building on your left (there is a great view looking back).

Continue 150m further uphill to join a bend in a tarmac road that appears to go back right downhill and fork ahead left uphill which you take.

Follow the road for 130m to a sharp right bend where you take an old cobbled donkey track going off directly ahead uphill bearing left.

At the end of the 90m donkey track, reach another bend in that same tarmac road that appears to go back right downhill and ahead uphill which you take.

Continue following this tarmac road for 350m as it climbs and bears left and over a brow into the outskirts of Kefalas, reaching a junction at a bend in the main Xirosterni to Kefalas road going left downhill and ahead right uphill which you take.

Carefully cross over the road. Continue ahead 70m, going round a right bend, then take the lane forking off ahead left uphill, leaving the main road going off to the right.

Continue along this lane for 110m to take a fork ahead right over a brow. Follow the lane a further 140m as it snakes round three bends (right–left-right) to arrive at steel gates leading into the grounds of the main church.

Pass through the grounds of the church, leaving through the gates at the opposite side, to arrive in Kefalas square where there are some excellent tavernas in the vicinity for refreshments.

To continue the walk retrace you steps back through the church grounds, leaving through the steel gates. Continue ahead, back down the lane, to bear left and after only 5m take the lane that forks right uphill.

After 20m come to a turning off right uphill and a fork ahead left slightly uphill which you take, passing Villa Jasmine on the left. Follow the lane a short distance bearing right to a T-junction going right uphill and left downhill which you take.

Crete Walks in the Apokoronas

Follow this lane as it bears round to the left, ignoring a fork back right uphill, then passing a large plane tree on your right.

Continue 700m along the main course of this delightfully tranquil track (with great views), ignoring along the way two tracks off to the left, to reach a fork ahead right bearing right and a fork ahead left bearing right which you take.

Continue 500m along the main course of this gravel track, passing through any stock fences you might encounter along the way, as it gets narrower and rougher meandering downhill.

The last 100m are over loose rocks so please exercise due care and attention.

Reach the bottom of the track where there is a development of stone houses on the right with three prominent solar water tanks. Follow the track that goes ahead down left passing these properties.

Continue 140m to reach a fork back left bearing left, in front of a nice stone wall, which you ignore to take the fork ahead slightly right downhill.

After 230m, reach a tarmac road that goes back right downhill and ahead left uphill which you take.

Follow this road for 170m, as it goes over a brow and down to a road junction at the bottom of a dip where you continue ahead uphill, ignoring the two roads off to the left and right.

Follow the main course of this minor road as it bears round some bends with yellow arrows painted in the road that point in the opposite direction you are going, before going out of Xirosterni village.

After a further 230m you reach the junction with the main Xirosterni to Kefalas road going ahead left and back right, with the small church opposite that was the starting point of the walk.